P9-BJC-612

ERNST LUBITSCH'S
NINOTCHKA
STARRING
GRETA GARBO
MELVYN DOUGLAS

Edited by Richard J. Anobile

A DARIEN HOUSE BOOK

UNIVERSE BOOKS
NEW YORK

A DARIEN HOUSE BOOK

© Copyright 1975 Darien House, Inc.

Pictures and dialogue from the feature
motion picture NINOTCHKA used with
permission of and by special arrangement
with Metro-Goldwyn-Mayer, Inc.

The motion picture NINOTCHKA
© Copyright 1939 Loew's Incorporated;
Renewed 1966 Metro-Goldwyn-Mayer, Inc.

UNIVERSE BOOKS
381 Park Avenue South
New York, N.Y. 10016

Library of Congress Catalog Card Number: 75-4264

First Printing, April 1975.

ISBN 0 87663 219 3

Printed in the United States of America

1932

*"Greta, vy don't you tell those idiots
in your studio to let us do a picture together?
Gott, how I would love to direct a picture vith you!"*

*"You tell them, Ernst. I'm far too tired to talk
to studio executives."**

Seven years later, on May 19, 1939, that conversation became reality. Shooting commenced, and fifty-eight days later it was completed. NINOTCHKA was voted one of 1939's ten best films and Lubitsch had done it "again."

Many factors combine to make NINOTCHKA a classic, not the least of which is Garbo. But let me first touch on the direction and the writing.

Usually it is difficult to distinguish script from direction in motion pictures. What we see on screen is a combination of both. Unless the viewer can refer to a script it is unlikely that one could ever divorce what was written from what was directionally creative.

Screenwriters are an anonymous breed. They slave away pumping out revision upon revision, all at the behest of the director or the producer. And in the end their film becomes the director's picture or, even worse, the star's picture. Just how many names of screenwriters come to your mind?

As the director becomes more and more a central figure in film, the collaborative aspects of the art are forgotten. Yet only when there is complete cooperation between screenwriter and director can a well-constructed film be created. The creative processes of film-making must not be at odds within a production. Egos must be deposited at the studio gate.

To his credit, Lubitsch habitually collaborated closely with his screenwriters. There were never any surprises for Lubitsch or, for that matter, anyone involved on a Lubitsch film. NINOTCHKA was no exception.

Three of Hollywood's finest screenwriters, Charles Brackett, Billy Wilder and Walter Reisch, combined their wits to produce a concise screenplay which is perfectly paced and intelligently written. The film is full of numerous references to its own lines. The audience is continually forced to recall earlier dialogue and the effect is that one has fond memories of genuinely likeable characters. In addition, the screenplay is perfectly balanced so that sides are not drawn due to politics, but rather to personalities.

Lubitsch is all over the project. He obviously chose the original story as it was in line with all the elements of life he loved to rib. Here might be one of the keys to that Lubitsch touch. NINOTCHKA gave Lubitsch an opportunity to satirize sex, society and politics all in one stroke of the camera. Each of these elements, with few notable exceptions, are dealt with continually over the director's career.

NINOTCHKA typifies the style of film audiences craved in the '30s. One must suspend reality to completely enter the film's world. Despite all the maneuverings of the characters and their 'grave' problems, it is readily apparent that neither of them really have a care in the world. They never work, yet they constantly sip champagne and frequent nightclubs. All this might have finally run the film into boredom but for one very intangible element: Garbo.

She has been quoted as stating that NINOTCHKA is the only film of her career where she had a real director. I take exception to this and would like to point out that she was directed by Rouben Mammoulian in QUEEN CHRISTINA in 1933. Certainly, one cannot compare Lubitsch and Mammoulian. Each had their own very definite directorial style. Yet, if I had to choose between the two, I'd have to lean towards Mammoulian who brought an inventive curiosity to film which

---

*Used by permission from "The Lubitsch Touch" by Herman G. Weinberg

eventually led him into many pioneering concepts.

Lubitsch's direction of NINOTCHKA is plain and unobtrusive. He has a sense of scene—and the film is basically only a series of prolonged scenes, but one would be hard pressed to consider his style cinematic. Lubitsch's NINOTCHKA could easily have been a stage play. For an interesting comparison I would recommend seeing Mammoulian's last film, the 1957 remake of NINOTCHKA, the musical SILK STOCKINGS. But I must also point out here that as the Lubitsch film was dominated by a strong screen personality, so too was Mammoulian's film dominated by Fred Astaire.

But let me get back to Garbo. I was stunned by her person. From the moment she enters the film in the second reel NINOTCHKA glows with a quality most rare in screen history. Even when I had reduced the film to the sixteen-hundred frame blowup photos I could not avoid her mysterious quality. Whatever that quality, it completely overshadows her acting. I can't help

feeling anger for the fact that the last time Garbo appeared on screen was in 1941. We all were cheated.

I keep feeling that I should be able to talk about her performance. But it is impossible. Garbo's performance, in any of her films, is herself. The power of that "performance" is that it is not being manufactured, it is real.

NINOTHCKA is a classic. It is a good example of fine screenwriting and it represents the quintessence of Lubitsch. But beyond that, it is Garbo. And if this record of NINOTCHKA works, every reader should be able to feel a discernible tingle through their body as Garbo works her powers.

RICHARD J. ANOBILE
New York City
February, 1975

Note to reader:

In keeping as true to the film as possible I have left in lap dissolves and fades where I felt they were necessary. The effect of a lap dissolve to the reader will be the appearance of two seemingly superimposed photos. The purpose here – as it was the director's, is to bridge the time and place gap between two scenes.

You will also notice a fuzziness in some frames. This is due to the fact that every photo is taken from blow-ups of the film itself. All possible means have been taken to insure clarity but inconsistencies in negative quality account for the variations of photo densities you will observe.

ACKNOWLEDGMENTS

I would like to take this opportunity to thank those individuals and corporations who helped to make this book possible.

The rights to produce this book were granted to us by Metro-Goldwyn-Mayer, Inc. Mr. Edward DeRista of the Dirco Corp. put a lot of time and effort into seeing to it that the rights were cleared. Once we were given the go-ahead, Mr. Mel Rydell saw to it that all the necessary materials made their way to New York from the vast MGM storage vaults.

Alyne Model, George Norris and Jan Kohn of Riverside Film Associates once again accurately transferred my frame selections to the negative materials. The blow-ups were produced by the Vita Print Corp. in New York under the watchful eye of Mr. Saul Jaffe.

Harry Chester Associates was once again responsible for the design. And Helen Garfinkle at Darien House saw to it that I remained co-ordinated.

Richard J. Anobile

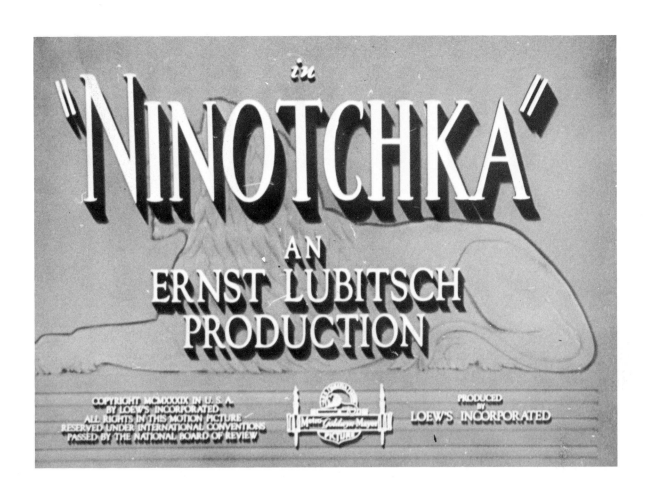

9

Screen Play by

CHARLES BRACKETT,
BILLY WILDER
and WALTER REISCH

Based on the Original Story by

MELCHIOR LENGYEL

Musical Score	WERNER R. HEYMANN
Recording Director	DOUGLAS SHEARER
Art Director	CEDRIC GIBBONS
Associate	RANDALL DUELL
Set Decorations	EDWIN B. WILLIS
Gowns by	ADRIAN
Make-Up Created by	JACK DAWN
Hair Styles for Miss Claire by	SYDNEY GUILAROFF
Director of Photography	WILLIAM DANIELS, A. S. C.
Film Editor	GENE RUGGIERO

Western Electric
SOUND SYSTEM

THIS PICTURE TAKES PLACE IN PARIS IN THOSE WONDERFUL DAYS WHEN A SIREN WAS A BRUNETTE AND NOT AN ALARM ... AND IF A FRENCHMAN TURNED OUT THE LIGHT IT WAS NOT ON ACCOUNT OF AN AIR RAID!

Manager: Is there anything I can do for you, Monsieur?
Buljanoff: No—no, no.

Manager: Yes, Monsieur?
Iranoff: Just looking around.

Kopalski: Comrades, why should we lie to each other? It's wonderful.

Iranoff: Let's be honest. Have we anything like it in Russia?
Kopalski and Buljanoff: No, no.
Iranoff: Can you imagine what the beds would be in a hotel like that?

Kopalski: They tell me when you ring once, the valet comes in. When you ring twice, you get a waiter. And do you know what happens when you ring three times?

Kopalski: A maid comes in — a French maid.

Iranoff: Comrades, if we ring nine times—!

Iranoff: Let's go in!
Buljanoff: Just a minute . . .

Buljanoff: . . . just a minute. I have nothing against the idea, but I still say, let's go back to the Hotel Terminus. Moscow made our reservations there. We are on an official mission, and we have no right to change the orders of our superiors.

Iranoff: Where is your courage, Comrade Buljanoff?

Kopalski: Are you the Buljanoff who fought on the barricades? And now you are afraid to take a room with a bath!
Buljanoff: I don't want to go to Siberia.

Iranoff: And I don't want to go to the Hotel Terminus!
Buljanoff: And I don't want to go to Siberia!

Buljanoff: No, no—no.

Iranoff: Buljanoff, listen to me.
Kopalski: Look, look—look, Buljanoff, if Lenin were alive he would say, "Buljanoff, Comrade, for once in your life you're in Paris. Don't be a fool. Go in there and ring three times."

Iranoff: He wouldn't say that. What he would say is, "Buljanoff, you can't afford to live in a cheap hotel. Doesn't the prestige of the Bolsheviks mean anything to you? Do you want to live in a hotel where you press for the hot water and cold water comes, and when you press for the cold water nothing comes at all? Phooey, Buljanoff."

21

Buljanoff: I still say our place is with the common people, but who am I to contradict Lenin? Let's go in!

Kopalski: Are you the manager?
Manager: Yes, Monsieur.
Kopalski: Pardon me for introducing Comrade Iranoff, member of the Russian Board of Trade.
Manager: Monsieur.

Iranoff: This is Comrade Kopalski.
Manager: Monsieur.

Buljanoff: And I am Comrade Buljanoff.
Manager: Monsieur.
Buljanoff: May I ask you, how much your rooms are?
Manager: Well, Gentlemen, I'm afraid our rates are rather high.

Buljanoff: Why should you be afraid? Why should he?
Manager: Well, I might be able to accommodate you. Is there some more luggage?

Iranoff: Oh, yes. But have you a safe big enough to hold this?

Manager: I'm afraid we have no boxes of that size in the vault, but there's a suite with a private safe.
Iranoff: That's even better.
Manager: But, Gentlemen, I'm afraid—

Buljanoff: He's always afraid.

Manager: I just wanted to explain! The apartment may suit your convenience, but I doubt whether it will fit your convictions. It's the Royal Suite.

Buljanoff: The Royal Suite?
Iranoff: Oh.
Buljanoff: Just a minute.

Buljanoff: Comrades, I warn you, if it gets out in Moscow that we stay in the Royal Suite, we'll get into terrible trouble.

Iranoff: We'll just tell them we had to do it on account of the safe. That's a perfect excuse. There was no other place big enough.
Kopalski: That's right.
Buljanoff: That's fine—that's fine.
Iranoff: Yes, yes.

Buljanoff: But, of course, we could take out the pieces and distribute them in three or four boxes in the vault and take a small room. That's an idea, isn't it?
Iranoff: Yes, that's an idea.

Iranoff: But who said we had to have an idea?
Kopalski: That's right. That's very good.

Buljanoff: Give us the Royal Suite!

Manager: Step this way, please.

Iranoff: Hello. Please connect me with Mercier.—Yes, the jeweler.

Iranoff: Hello. — No, I want to speak to Monsieur Mercier, personally.

Iranoff: Yes. Hello, Monsieur Mercier? This is Iranoff, Member of the Russian Board of Trade. — Yes, we arrived this morning.

Iranoff: Oh, thank you, very, very much. Yes, we have everything here. — The necklace, too. All fourteen pieces. — At the — What?

Iranoff: No, Monsieur Mercier. The court jewels of the Grand Duchess Swana consisted of fourteen pieces. Why don't you check on that? — Of course, we have all the necessary credentials.

Rakonin: Will you take care of the Royal Suite? I will be back in ten minutes.
Waiter: All right, Rakonin.
Rakonin: Thank you very much. Thank you.

Rakonin: Eight Rue de Chalon.
Driver: Bien, Monsieur.

Swana: Hello, Leon.
Leon: Good morning, Swana, darling.

Swana: Oh, it's really a wretched morning —wretched! I can't get myself right. I wanted to look mellow, and I look brittle.

Swana: My face doesn't compose well.

Swana: It's all highlights! How can I dim myself down, Leon? Suggest something.

Swana: Oh, I'm so bored with this face! I wish I had someone else's face. Whose face would you have if you had your choice? Oh, well, I guess one gets the face one deserves.

Leon: There's one marvelous advantage to your composition, Swana. However many questions you ask, you never expect an answer.
Swana: Don't you find that restful?
Leon: Um-hmm.

Swana: Good morning, darling.
Leon: Good morning.

Swana: Why didn't you come last night?
Leon: Darling, I was looking after your interests.
Swana: Oh, did you win?

Leon: We can forget horse racing, roulette, everything.

Leon: Our worries are over.

Leon: You remember the platinum watch with the diamond numbers? You'll be in a position to give it to me now.

Swana: Oh, darling, you're so good to me.

Leon: We could be rich, if you say the word. I had dinner with the Guizots last night.
Swana: Oh, those awful newspaper people!

Leon: You'd be surprised how many nice people dine with the Guizots.
Swana: What a gruesome proof of the power of the press.
Leon: Now listen, Swana. I sold Monsieur Guizot the idea of publishing your memoirs in the Gazette Parisienne.

Swana: What!
Leon: "The Life and Loves of the Grand Duchess Swana of Russia."
Swana: Oh, Leon!
Leon: But, darling, we won't have to worry about our future, if you're willing to raffle off your past.

Swana: Come in.

Maid: Count Rakonin asks the privilege of a few words, Your Highness.
Leon: Rakonin?
Swana: Yes. He's a waiter at the Clarence, poor devil. You know him.
Leon: Oh, yes.

Swana: Well, tell him I'm sorry. I won't be able to see him for half an hour.
Maid: The Count says if it could be as soon as possible. It's luncheon time, and he is just between courses.
Swana: All right, all right. I'll see him right away.

Swana: But I can't get myself right today!

Swana: Highlights—
Leon: Darling, Count Rakonin's between courses.

Swana: Oh, yes. My Little Volga Boatman!
Leon: Ummm.

Swana: How do you do, my friend.

Rakonin: Your Highness.
Swana: Won't you sit down?

Rakonin: Your Highness, forgive this intrusion—
Swana: What's the matter, Rakonin? Have you lost your job?

Rakonin: No, Madame. Something of the utmost importance.
It concerns your jewels.

Swana: My jewels?
Rakonin: I remember one birthday of His Majesty, our beloved
Czar, I had the honor of being on guard at his summer palace.
I still see you bending before His Majesty. You wore your
diadem and a necklace.

Swana: But why do you bring this up after all these years?
Rakonin: They are here. Your jewels, here in Paris!

Swana: Alexis, do you know what you're saying?
Rakonin: This morning three Soviet agents arrived. I overheard a telephone conversation with Mercier, the jeweler. Your Highness, they're going to sell them!

Leon: Did I hear something about jewels?

Swana: Rakonin, bless him, has just given me the most amazing news! You know Count d'Algout.
Rakonin: How do you do, Monsieur.
Swana: I will call my lawyer at once.

Rakonin: I am sorry, Your Highness. I have to leave.

Swana: Oh, thank you, my dear friend. I'll get in touch with you.
Rakonin: Au revoir, Your Highness.
Swana: Hello. Balzac 2-7-6-9.

Rakonin: Au revoir, Monsieur.
Leon: Au revoir.

Swana: This is the Grand Duchess Swana. I want to speak to Monsieur Cornillon. It's very important. Please get him right away. — Hello, Monsieur Cornillon? The most incredible thing has happened. My jewels are here in Paris! Three Bolshevik swine are trying to sell them. — Yes. Yes. Now — now, we must act immediately. Call the police! Have them arrested! — Well then, get an injunction! — But do something, Monsieur Cornillon! — But they are my jewels! There must be some way of getting them back!

Leon: What does he say?
Swana: But how can there be a question? Are you my lawyer, or theirs? Oh. Yes, all right. Yes, all right. I'll — I'll call you later.

Leon: What did he say?
Swana: Oh, it looks pretty hopeless. There may be a chance, that's all.

Swana: The French Government has recognized Soviet Russia, and he doubts that they will risk a war for my poor sake. He might be able to make up some kind of case, but it would cost money.

Swana: Money, money! That's all they are interested in, those lawyers!

Leon: Darling, calm down. Calm down. Why do you need a lawyer? Haven't you your little Volga Boatman?

Mercier: Very good, excellent, superb. It'd be foolish to belittle the quality of the merchandise, but your terms are impossible. My counteroffer is the absolute maximum.
Kopalski: But, Monsieur Mercier—

Mercier: Now, now, gentlemen, I'm going to let you in on a little secret. We are undertaking this deal only because of the prestige involved. And frankly, we're expecting to take a loss.

Iranoff: Capitalistic methods.
Buljanoff: Hmmm. They accumulate millions by taking loss after loss.

Buljanoff: This is Buljanoff, Iranoff and Kopalski.—Who? Count d'Algout? No . . . no, that must be a mistake. No—we can't be disturbed.

Mercier: I can assure you that no one else can meet the figure named by my syndicate—at least, not under the present economic conditions.
Kopalski: We can wait.

Iranoff: Do we give the impression of people who are pressed for money?
Mercier: Yes. Come, gentlemen, let's put our cards on the table.

Mercier: Right now there is a Russian commission in New York trying to sell fifteen Rembrandts; there is another in London mortgaging the oil fields in Baku. You need money, and you need it quickly. Now, I think my offer is a very fair one and doesn't even take advantage of your situation.

Kopalski: Just a minute.

Iranoff: Now, listen . . .
Buljanoff: Wait, just a minute.

Buljanoff: The pieces are all registered.
Mercier: Yes, I know. Thank you so much.

Iranoff: He's cutting our throats.
Buljanoff: What can we do? We have to accept.
Kopalski: Comrades—comrades—Don't let's give in so quickly.
After all, we have to uphold the prestige of Russia.

Buljanoff: All right, let's uphold it for another ten minutes.
Iranoff: Yes.

Iranoff: We don't want to be disturbed.
Leon: My name is d'Algout. I telephoned.
Iranoff: If you want to see us, you must come in later.

Leon: I just want a word with Monsieur Mercier.
Iranoff: You can't come in here.

Leon: Monsieur Mercier—may I introduce myself? I am Leon d'Algout. I think I had the pleasure of meeting you in your beautiful shop.

Leon: I was admiring the platinum watch with the diamond numbers.
Mercier: Oh, yes . . . yes, of course.
Leon: You remember, I—Oh,

Leon: glorious, aren't they?

Kopalski: Now, M'sieur, you have no right . . .
Iranoff: I did not permit you to come in here.
Leon: Just a moment.

Leon: I hope you haven't closed this deal, M'sieur Mercier. It might bring you into serious trouble.
Iranoff: Who are you and what do you want?

Leon: Those jewels were the property of the Grand Duchess Swana, and were seized illegally by the Soviet Government. I am acting for Her Highness. Here is my Power of Attorney.

Iranoff: You know, M'sieur Mercier, this is all nonsense.
Kopalski: These may have been the jewels of the Grand Duchess Swana, but like all private property, they were confiscated by the state.

Leon: We'll leave the problem of their ownership to the French courts. In the meanwhile, gentlemen, I have filed a petition for an injunction to prohibit you from either selling or removing the jewels.

Leon: Here is a copy. If there is anything in the petition which isn't clear, gentlemen, I shall be glad to explain it.

Mercier: Thank you.

Mercier: Well, gentlemen, this introduces a new element into our negotiations. Until this claim is completely settled . . .
Kopalski: We can call our ambassador.

Iranoff: I give you my word, they were confiscated legally.
Kopalski and Buljanoff: That's right! That's right!

Mercier: Oh, now, now, gentlemen. Please try to understand my position. I am not withdrawing. My offer stands. And when you can produce a clear title, approved by the French Courts, we can close the deal. Until then, gentlemen, good day.

Leon: I thought it my duty to warn you.

Leon: I should have hated to see you get into trouble, M'sieur.
Mercier: Thank you. Thank you.
Leon: I hope you will forgive me.
Mercier: On the contrary. I consider myself very lucky. Good day.
Leon: Good day, M'sieur.

Buljanoff: You believe me, I—

Leon: Well, gentlemen, how about a little lunch?

Iranoff: Ah—you! Will you get out of here!
Buljanoff: Yes!
Kopalski: Get out!
Leon: But don't look so gloomy, gentlemen. You may have a chance.

Kopalski: We may have a chance!
Iranoff: Ha! Ridiculous!

Leon: Yes, a very slim one. I want to be fair. I don't deny that you might make out some kind of a case.
Kopalski: We haven't anything to discuss with you.
Buljanoff: No.
Kopalski: You talk to a lawyer.

Iranoff: Lawyer!
Buljanoff: Yes—lawyer!

Leon: All right, you talk to a lawyer and I'll talk to a judge.
Iranoff: Well, that won't help you. You can't intimidate us.

Kopalski: Soviet Russia will put all its might behind this case.

Buljanoff: Yes. You think because you represent the former Grand Duchess—
Leon: The Grand Duchess!
Buljanoff: The former Grand Duchess.

45

Leon: At any rate, gentlemen, a charming, exquisite woman.
Leon: I warn you, gentlemen, if this case comes to trial, it will be before a French court. And when the Grand Duchess takes the stand—
Iranoff: All right, go ahead, get her on the witness stand. What can she say?

Leon: But how will she look? The fashions this spring are very becoming to her.

Leon: Oh, gentlemen, the judge will be French, the jury will be French, everybody in the courtroom will be French. Have you ever seen a French court when a beautiful woman sits on the witness stand and raises her skirt a little? You sit down and pull up your pants and where would it get you?

Iranoff: I suppose you expect us to hand over the jewels, huh?
Leon: Oh, no, no—I'm not a highwayman, just a nuisance. All I want to do is make things as difficult as possible.

Buljanoff: Uh—not that we are giving in one inch, but tell us what is in your mind?
Iranoff: Yeah.

Leon: Well, gentlemen, what about my proposition?
Iranoff: What proposition?
Leon: I just said—let's have some lunch.

Iranoff, Buljanoff, Kopalski: Ahh!

Iranoff, Buljanoff, Kopalski: Ah-ah!

Iranoff, Buljanoff, Kopalski: AH-AHH!

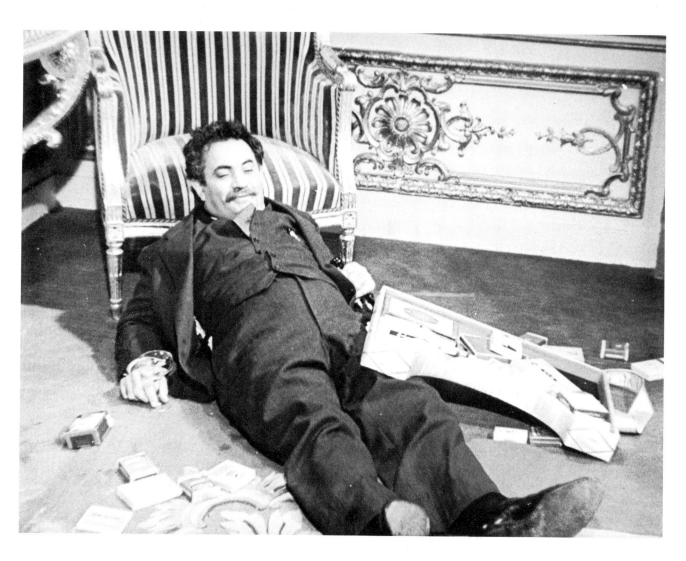

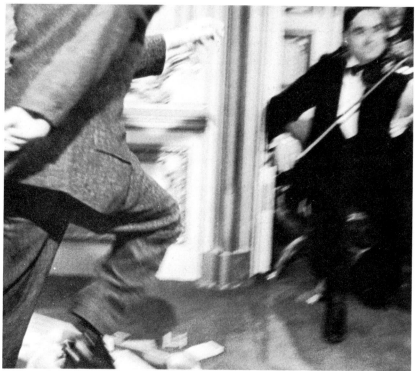

Leon: Hey, Sascha! Serge! Mischa!

Iranoff: Oh, d'Algout—what is it, my boy?
Buljanoff: Leon—what do you want?

51

Iranoff: Uh—what can we do for you, Leon.
Leon: It's about that telegram to Moscow. Why should you bother about it? I've written it for you.

Buljanoff: Oh, Leon, Leonitchka. Why are you so good to us?

Buljanoff: Why are you so good to us?
Leon: That's very nice, boys. Now, wait a minute, wait a minute, boys. Wait a minute.

Leon: What was the name of that Commissar of the Board of Trade?
Iranoff: Razinin.

Leon: Razinin. Commissar Razinin, Board of Trade, Moscow.
Kopalski: You wouldn't like Razinin.
Buljanoff: No, he's a bad man. He sends people to Siberia.
Iranoff: We don't like Razinin.
Buljanoff: No—no!
Iranoff: No, we don't like him.

Buljanoff: We like Leon. Don't we like Leon?
Kopalski: Oh, yes—we like Leon. Yes—yes!
Leon: Wait a minute!

Leon: Wait a minute. Wait a minute. Now wait a minute — how's this?

Leon: "Commissar Razinin, Board of Trade, Moscow. Unexpected situation here. Grand Duchess Swana in Paris claims jewels and has already brought injunction against sale or removal.

Leon: After long and serious study, we suggest in the interest of our beloved country a fifty-fifty settlement as best solution. Iranoff, Buljanoff and Kopalski!"
Kopalski: If we send that, Leon, we'll be sent to Siberia.

Iranoff: And if we have to go to Siberia . . .
Leon: I'll send you a muff.

Buljanoff: Leon, why are you so good to us?

Iranoff: Yes!
Kopalski: Leonitchka!

Buljanoff: Comrade Waiter!
Kopalski: Oh, Waiter—Dear Waiter!

Iranoff: Why are you so good to us?
Kopalski: Why are you so good to us?

Leon: That's enough. Get back to the other room. Enough—enough—go along.

Leon: Take this to the telegraph office at once.
Rakonin: Yes, M'sieur.

54

Iranoff: Hello.—Yes, Leon. What is it, Leon?—Oh, you can't hurry such things. You must give Moscow a little time. There's nothing we can do about it. Why don't you drop in later?—Yes. Au revoir.

Buljanoff: Mischa! Mischa!
Iranoff: What's the matter?

Buljanoff: Uh—this telegram from Moscow. It must have been here all day.

Iranoff: "Halt negotiations immediately. Envoy Extraordinary arrives Thursday 5:20 P.M. with full power. Your authority cancelled herewith. Razinin."

Iranoff: It is Thursday.
Buljanoff: It's five o'clock already.
Kopalski: I always said it would be Siberia.

Iranoff: Come on.

Iranoff: Give me the desk, please. This . . . this is the Royal Suite. Iranoff speaking. Listen, a special envoy is coming from Moscow today. He'll occupy the Royal Suite. Move our things to the smallest room you've got. — Yes, right away! Instantly!

Trainman: Pass, please?

Iranoff: Now this is a fine thing. Maybe we've missed him already.
Kopalski: How can we find somebody without knowing what he looks like?

Iranoff: That must be the one!

Buljanoff: Yes, he looks like a Comrade.
Iranoff: Yes.

Man: Heil Hitler!
Woman: Heil Hitler!

Iranoff: No, that's not him.
Buljanoff: Positively not.

Iranoff: What are we going to do now?
Buljanoff: I don't know.
Iranoff: We . . . we must have missed him.

58

Ninotchka: I am looking for Michael Simonovitch Iranoff.

Iranoff: I am Michael Simonovitch Iranoff.

Ninotchka: I am Nina Ivanovna Yakushova, Envoy Extraordinary, acting under direct orders of Comrade Commissar Razinin.

Ninotchka: Present me to your colleagues.

Iranoff: Comrade Buljanoff.
Ninotchka: Comrade.

Iranoff: Comrade Kopalski.
Ninotchka: Comrade.

Iranoff: What a charming idea for Moscow to surprise us with a lady Comrade.

Kopalski: If we had known we would have greeted you with flowers.
Iranoff: Ahh, yes.

Ninotchka: Don't make an issue of my womanhood.

Ninotchka: We are here for work, all of us. Let's not waste any time. Shall we go?

Iranoff: Porter!

Porter: Here, please.
Ninotchka: What do you want?
Porter: May I have your bags, Madame?
Ninotchka: Why?

Kopalski: He is a porter. He wants to carry them.

Ninotchka: Why? Why should you carry other people's bags?
Porter: Well, that's my business, Madame.
Ninotchka: That's no business. That's social injustice.

Porter: That depends on the tip.
Kopalski: Allow me, Comrade.
Ninotchka: No. No, thank you.

First Trainman: Tickets, please.
Second: Tickets. please.
Third: Tickets.

Buljanoff: How are things in Moscow?
Ninotchka: Very good. The last mass trials were a great success.
There are going to be fewer but better Russians!

64

Ninotchka: What's that?

Kopalski: It's a hat, Comrade. A woman's hat.

Ninotchka: How can such a civilization survive which permits their women to put things like that on their heads?

Ninotchka: It won't be long now, Comrades.

Buljanoff: This is the apartment we have reserved for you, Comrade Yakushova. I hope you like it.

Ninotchka: Which part of the room is mine?

Iranoff: You see, Comrade, it's a little different here. They don't rent rooms in pieces.

Iranoff: We had to take the whole suite.

Ninotchka: How much does this cost?
Iranoff: Two thousand francs.
Ninotchka: A week?
Iranoff: A day.

Ninotchka: Do you know how much a cow costs, Comrade Iranoff?
Iranoff: A cow?

Ninotchka: Two thousand francs. If I stay here a week I will cost the Russian people seven cows.

Ninotchka: Who am I to cost the Russian people seven cows?

Buljanoff: We had to take it on account of the safe.
Iranoff: For ourselves, we are much happier now since we moved to a little room right next to the servants quarters.

Ninotchka: I'm ashamed to put a picture of Lenin in a room like this.

Iranoff: Do you want to be alone, Comrade?
Ninotchka: No.

Ninotchka: Comrades, your telegram was received with great disfavor in Moscow.
Kopalski: We did our best, Comrade.

Ninotchka: I hope so for your sake. Let's examine the case. What does the lawyer say?
Buljanoff: Which lawyer?
Ninotchka: You didn't get legal advice?

Kopalski: We dealt directly with the representative of the Grand Duchess. I am sure if we call him he will give you a very clear picture.

Ninotchka: I will not repeat your mistake. I will have no dealings with the Grand Duchess nor her representatives.

Ninotchka: Comrade Buljanoff?

Buljanoff: Yes, Comrade.

Ninotchka: Do you spell Buljanoff with one or two f's?

Buljanoff: With two f's if you please.

Ninotchka: Have you some cigarettes?

Iranoff: This is the Royal Suite. Please send up some cigarettes.

Iranoff: You just telephone and you get what you want. That's the capitalistic system.

Ninotchka: Comrades, I am not in a position to pass final judgment but at best you've been careless in your duty to the State.

Ninotchka: You were entrusted with more than a mere sale of jewelry. Why are we peddling our precious possessions to the world at this time? Our next years crop is in danger and you know it!

Ninotchka: Unless we can get foreign currency to buy tractors, there'll not be enough bread for our people.

Ninotchka: And you, Comrades—
Kopalski: We did it with the best intentions.

Ninotchka: We can't feed the Russian people on your intentions. Fifty per cent to a so-called Grand Duchess. Half of every loaf of bread to our enemy.

Ninotchka: Comrade Kopalski.
Kopalski: Yes, Comrade?
Ninotchka: Go at once to our embassy and get me the address of the best lawyer in Paris.
Kopalski: Yes, Comrade.

Ninotchka: And you, Comrade Iranoff, go to the public library and get me the section of the civil code of properties.

Buljanoff: Is there anything I can do, Comrade.
Ninotchka: Yes, you might get me an accurate map of Paris. I want to use my spare time to inspect public utilities. And to make a study of all outstanding technical achievements in the city.
Buljanoff: Yes, Comrade.

Ninotchka: Come in.

First girl: Hello.
Second girl: Hello, cigarettes?
Third girl: Hello.

Ninotchka: Comrades, you must have been smoking a lot.

Clerk: Desk. — Yes, Monsieur Kopalski. — You are expecting Count D'Algout. — Uh-huh. — But he is not to go to the Royal Suite under any circumstances. He should go to your new room, nine-eight-five. Thank you, Monsieur.

Ninotchka: You, please.
Leon: Hm? Me?
Ninotchka: Could you give me some information?

Leon: Oh, gladly.

Ninotchka: How long must we wait here?
Leon: Well, a—until the policeman blows his whistle again.
Ninotchka: At what intervals does he whistle?
Leon: What?

Ninotchka: How many minutes between the first and second whistle?
Leon: Well, you know, that's very funny. I never thought of that before.
Ninotchka: You've never been caught in a similar situation?

Leon: Yes, I have. Now that I come to think about it, it's staggering. Good heavens! If I add it all up, I must have spent years waiting for signals. Imagine an important part of my life wasted between whistles.

Ninotchka: In other words, you don't know?
Leon: No.
Ninotchka: Thank you.

Leon: You're welcome.

Leon: Can I be of any assistance to you?

Ninotchka: You might hold this for me.
Leon: I'd love to.

Ninotchka: Correct me if I am wrong. We are facing North, aren't we?

Leon: Facing North—well now, I—I'd hate to commit myself without my compass.

Leon: Pardon me, are you an explorer?
Ninotchka: No, I am looking for the Eiffel Tower.

Leon: A—good heavens, is that thing lost again? Oh are you interested in a view?

Ninotchka: I'm interested in the Eiffel Tower from a technical standpoint.

Leon: Technical? No, no, I'm afraid I couldn't be of much help from that angle. You see, a Parisian only goes to the Tower in moments of despair to jump off.

Ninotchka: How long does it take a man to land?
Leon: A—

Leon: Now isn't that too bad, the last time I jumped I forgot to time it.

Leon: Let me see now, the Eiffel tower—The—Ahh! Your finger, please.

Ninotchka: Why do you need my finger?

Leon: It's bad manners to point with your own.

Leon: There. The Eiffel Tower.
Ninotchka: And where are we?

Leon: Where are we? Now let me see, where are we? Now here we are. There you are and here am I. Feel it?

Ninotchka: I'm interested only in the shortest distance between these two points. Must you flirt?

Leon: Well, I don't have to but I find it natural.
Ninotchka: Surpress it.
Leon: I'll try.

Ninotchka: For my own information, would you call your approach toward me typical of the local morale?
Leon: Madamoiselle, it is that approach which has made Paris what it is.
Ninotchka: You're very sure of yourself, aren't you?

Leon: Well, nothing's happened recently to shake my self confidence.

Ninotchka: I have heard of the arrogant male in capitalistic society. It is having a superior earning power that makes you that way.

Leon: A Russian! I love Russians! Comrade, I've been fascinated by your Five Year Plan for the last fifteen years.

Ninotchka: Your type will soon be extinct.

Leon: Taxi!

Ninotchka: Can you tell me the exact width of the foundation on which these piers are resting, and the depth?
Attendant: You don't have to worry —the thing is safe.
Ninotchka: I am not afraid, I just want to—

Leon: "The foundation is one hundred and forty-one yards square."

Leon: I hope you'll forgive me but I thought you'd—
Ninotchka: Go on.

Leon: "Four massive pieces of masonry are sunk to a depth of forty-six feet on the side of the Seine, and twenty-nine and one-half feet on the other side. The girders of interlaced ironwork which stay the structure have an inclination of fifty-four degrees."

Ninotchka: That's a strange angle.
Leon: Yes, yes, very strange.

Leon: "Ascending to the first platform is a staircase consisting of —eight hundred and twenty-nine steps. A—

Leon: And an additional two hundred and fifty-four steps to the very top!

Leon: There's an elevator included in the price of admission! It'll take you hours to walk up there. The elevator will get you up in three minutes!

Ninotchka: You gave me some very valuable information. Thank you.
Leon: Thank you for getting me up here. I've never seen this before.

Leon: Beautiful, isn't it?
Ninotchka: Yes, it is.
Leon: I'm glad I saw it before becoming extinct.

Ninotchka: Now don't misunderstand me. I do not hold your frivolity against you. As basic material you may not be bad, but you are the unfortunate product of a doomed culture. I feel very sorry for you.

Leon: Oh, but you must admit that this doomed old civilization sparkles. Look at it!

Leon: It glitters.

Ninotchka: I do not deny its beauty, but it's a waste of electricity.

Leon: What a city! There are the Grands Boulevard, blasted out of the heart of the old city. The Arc de Triomphe, built to greet Napoleon's army. The Opera! Montparnasse! Montmartre!

Leon: And now, I'll show you the greatest attraction of all.

Leon: It'll cost me a franc but it's worth it. The most unique spot in all Paris. Really, I'm not exaggerating.

Leon: It's wonderful. It's charming. It's—

Leon: Ah, please.

Leon: What do you see?
Ninotchka: I see a house. Looks like any other house. What's remarkable about it?

Leon: Oh, it's not the structure. It's the spirit that dwells within it. It has three rooms and a kitchenette dedicated to hospitality.

Ninotchka: So it's your house?
Leon: Um, well, let's say I live in it.
Ninotchka: Hm.

Leon: It's such a pleasant little place. It has all the comforts. Easy to reach — near the subway, bus and street car.

Ninotchka: Does it mean you want me to go there?
Leon: Oh, now please, please, don't misunderstand me.
Ninotchka: Then you don't want me to go there?

Leon: No, no, no, no! No, no, I didn't say that either. Naturally nothing would please me more.
Ninotchka: Then why don't we go? You might be an interesting subject of study.

Leon: I'll do my best.

Leon: Good evening, Gaston.
Gaston: Good evening, Monsieur.
Ninotchka: Is this what you call the "butler"?
Leon: Yes.

Ninotchka: Good evening, comrade.

Ninotchka: This man is very old. You shouldn't make him work.
Leon: He takes good care of that.

Ninotchka: He looks sad. Do you whip him?
Leon: No, but the mere thought makes my mouth water.

Ninotchka: The day will come when you will be free. Go to bed, little father. We want to be alone.

Leon: Please.

Gaston: Count d'Algout, there have been several telephone calls.

Leon: Go to bed, little father.

Leon: Now, may I offer you a drink?

Ninotchka: Thank you, I'm not thirsty.
Leon: Well, perhaps something to eat.
Ninotchka: I've had all the calories necessary for today.

Leon: Oh, yes, all the calories.
Ninotchka: What do we do now?

Leon: Ahhhh, shall we have some music?
Ninotchka: Is that customary?

Leon: Hmmmm—it helps. It has ever since King David wooed Bathsheba with his harp. Not being so fortunate as to have my harp at hand, I'll turn on the radio.

Leon: If there's anything you'd like to study, please go ahead. I've nothing to conceal. This is my desk. These are my books, and here am I. Where shall we begin?

Ninotchka: I will start with you.
Leon: Excellent!

Leon: Now, let's see, I'm thirty-five years old, just over six feet tall, and weigh a hundred and eighty-two pounds stripped.

Ninotchka: What is your profession?
Leon: My profession? Mmmm—keeping my body fit, keeping my mind alert and keeping the landlord appeased. That's a full time job.

Ninotchka: And what do you do for mankind?
Leon: For mankind? Yes, a . . .

Leon: Not so much for mankind, but for womankind, my record isn't quite so bleak.

Ninotchka: You are something we do not have in Russia.

Leon: Thank you. Glad you told me.

Ninotchka: That's why I believe in the future of my country.
Leon: Yeah!

Leon: I'm beginning to believe in it myself, since I've met you—
I still don't—quite know what it's all about—it confuses me—
it frightens me, but it fascinates me.

Leon: Ninotchka, do you like me just a little bit?
Ninotchka: Your general appearance is not distasteful.
Leon: Thank you.
Ninotchka: The whites of your eyes are clear. Your cornea is
excellent.

Leon: Your cornea is terrific! Ninotchka, tell me—you're so expert on things—can it be that I'm falling in love with you?

Ninotchka: Why must you bring in wrong values? Love is a romantic designation for a most ordinary biological, or shall we say, chemical process.

Ninotchka: A lot of nonsense is talked and written about it.

Leon: Oh, I see. What do you use instead?
Ninotchka: I acknowledge the existence of a natural impulse common to all.

Leon: What can I possibly do to encourage such an impulse in you?
Ninotchka: You don't have to do a thing. Chemically we are already quite sympathetic.

Leon: You are the most incredible creature I've ever met. Ninotchka, Ninotchka, —
Ninotchka: You repeat yourself.
Leon: Yes, I'd like to say it a thousand times.

Leon: You must forgive me if I seem a little old-fashioned. After all I'm just a poor bourgeois.

Ninotchka: It's never too late to change. I used to belong to the petty bourgeoisie myself.
Leon: No!

Ninotchka: My father and mother wanted me to stay and work on the farm, but I preferred the bayonnet.
Leon: The bayonnet? Did you really?

Ninotchka: I was wounded before Warsaw.   **Leon:** Wounded, how?

Ninotchka: I was a Sergeant in the Third Cavalry Brigade. Would you like to see my wound?
Leon: I'd love to.

Ninotchka: A Polish lancer. I was sixteen.
Leon: Poor Ninotchka. Poor, poor Ninotchka.
Ninotchka: Don't pity me. Pity the Polish Lancer. After all, I'm still alive.

Leon: What kind of a girl are you anyway?
Ninotchka: Just what you see. A tiny cog in the great wheel of evolution.
Leon: You're the most adorable cog I've ever seen. Ninotchka, let me confess something. Never did I dream I could feel like this toward a Sergeant.

Leon: Do you hear that?

Ninotchka: It's twelve o'clock.

Leon: It's midnight. Look at the clock. One hand has met the other hand. They kiss. Isn't that wonderful?

Ninotchka: That's the way a clock works. What's wonderful about it?

Leon: Ninotchka, it's midnight. One half of Paris is making love to the other half.

Ninotchka: You merely feel you must put yourself in a romantic mood to add to your exhilaration.
Leon: I can't possibly think of any better reason.

Ninotchka: That's false sentimentality.

Leon: Oh, you analyze everything out of existence. You'd analyze me out of existence, but I won't let you. Love isn't so simple, Ninotchka.

Leon: Ninotchka, why do doves bill and coo? Why do snails, the coldest of all creatures, circle interminably around each other? Why do moths fly hundreds of miles to find their mates?

Leon: Why do flowers slowly open their petals? Oh, Ninotchka— Ninotchka, surely you feel some slight symptom of the divine passion.

Leon: A general warmth in the palms of your hands—a strange heaviness in your limbs.

Leon: A burning of the lips that isn't thirst but something a thousand times more tantalizing, more exalting, than thirst?

Ninotchka: You are very talkative.

Leon: Was that talkative?

Ninotchka: No. That was restful. Again!

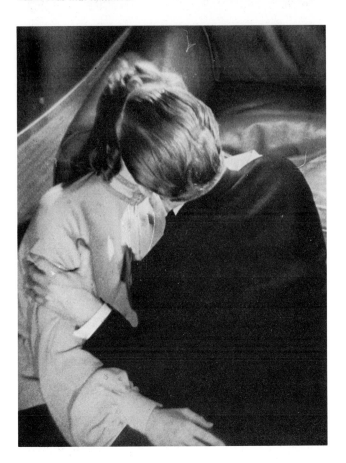

Ninotchka: Thank you.

Leon: Oh, my barbaric Ninotchka.

Leon: My impossible, unromantic, statistical, glo—

Leon: Again!
Ninotchka: The telephone is ringing.
Leon: Let it ring.
Ninotchka: One of your friends may be in need of you. You must answer.

Leon: Ohhhhh . . .

Leon: Ahh! Hello.—Yes.—What?—Oh, yes, well, I'm sorry I couldn't make it.—No, I ran into an old friend from the army.—What?—The whole deal is off! Are you crazy, Buljanoff?

Leon: Oh, oh, oh, a special envoy arrived? Huh?

Leon: I'll be glad to see her whenever she wants to.—She doesn't want to see me. Well, what do you know about that? Why?—Uh-huh. Well, I'll get in touch with her myself.

Leon: What's her name?—Huh? Yaku—good Heavens, these Russian names. How do you spell it?

Leon: I—oh, oh,—Y—Y. A. Yakushova.

Leon: Thanks.

Leon: Yakushova—Ninotchka!

Leon: Yes. All right, thank you.

Leon: Ninotchka!
Ninotchka: I must go.
Leon: Or shall I say Special Envoy Yakushova.

Ninotchka: Let's forget we ever met.

Leon: No, no, no, I have a much better suggestion.

Leon: Let's forget the telephone ever rang.

Leon: I never heard that you are Yakushova. You are Ninotchka, my Ninotchka!

Ninotchka: I was sent here by my country to fight you.

Leon: All right, fight me. Fight me as much as you want, only fight me tomorrow morning! There's nothing sweeter than sharing a secret with an enemy.
Ninotchka: You represent White Russia and I represent Red Russia.
Leon: No, no. Tonight let's not represent anybody but ourselves.

Ninotchka: It's out of the question. If you wish to approach me . . .
Leon: You know I want to.
Ninotchka: Then do it through my lawyer!

Leon: But, Ninotchka, you can't walk out like this. I'm crazy about you.

Leon: I thought I'd make an impression on you. You liked the whites of my eyes.

Ninotchka: I must go.

Leon: Oh, Ninotchka, I held you in my arms. You kissed me.

Ninotchka: I kissed the Polish Lancer, too . . .

Ninotchka: ...before he died.

Swana: Yes, Marianne, darling. No, you didn't waken me. I'm not only up—I'm on my way out.

Swana: Yes, I want to catch Leon, before he rushes out and loses himself in my business affairs. Oh, everything was going perfectly until three days ago when some horrid female envoy arrived from Moscow. Now, we don't know where we are.

Swana: Yes, I'll telephone you tonight, darling—goodbye, dear.

Lawyer: I seem to remember some additional injunctive provision dealing with the property of foreigners residing in France.

Ninotchka: You are referring to paragraph 59B, section 25f of the Civil Code.

Ninotchka: Page eight hundred and twenty-four. And do not fail to read the three footnotes.

Ninotchka: While you are studying it, I will eat.

Driver: Where to, Madame?
Ninotchka: Can you recommend a restaurant?
Driver: Well, there's Guengue's if you care for sea food.
Ninotchka: Where do you eat?
Driver: At Pere Mathieu's.
Ninotchka: Where is that?
Driver: Why, it's just a place for workmen.
Ninotchka: Where is it?
Driver: Down eight blocks. Rue de Paudel.
Ninotchka: Thank you.

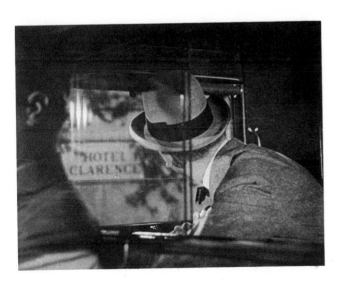

113

Pere: Are you alone, Madame? A nice little corner table? Or perhaps by the window would be better?

Pere: This way, Madame.

Pere: I think this is the first time you've been in my little place. Your face is new to me.

Pere: Now what shall it be?

Ninotchka: Raw beets and carrots.

Pere: Madame, this is a restaurant, not a meadow. Now here's what we are offering today. Please make your choice. I'm sure you will find something to tempt your appetite.

Leon: Well, for goodness sake, hello.

Leon: Well, it certainly is a small world, isn't it?

Pere: Well, Madame? Shall we start with soup? Fish soup today. I got up at five to fish them from the Seine.

Leon: Ah—crayfish soup for me!
Pere: Very well, M'sieur.

Pere: Then, may I suggest an omelet with mushrooms?
Ninotchka: Bring me something simple. I never think about food.

Pere: Madame, if you don't think about food, what do you think about?
Ninotchka: The future of the common people.
Pere: That's also a question of food. I will bring you a nice little lunch a la Pere Mathieu.

Leon: May I say something? You insulted him, do you know that? You hurt his feelings. Well, it's just like telling a musician that you don't like music.

Leon: Why, that good old man believes in food just as you believe in Karl Marx. You can't go around hurting people like that, Comrade Yakushova. But you can make it up to him.

Leon: Do you know how? By eating everything that he brings you with relish, by drinking everything with gusto, by having a good time for the first time in your natural life!

Ninotchka: I don't like you following me.

Leon: I didn't follow you.
Ninotchka: How did you get here?
Leon: I always eat here.
Ninotchka: This is a place for working-men.

Leon: But my dear child, I am most at home among working-men. I hate those places where you circulate, the Clarence Hotel and those places. This is my natural element. After all, what are any of us? Working-men! At least, those of us who are worth our salt.

Leon: Hi'ya!

Man: Hi!

Leon: Hi'Ya!
Man: Hi'ya!

Man: Hi!

Leon: Hi'ya, boys!
Men: Hi'ya.
Leon: How's everything today? Is the lunch all right?
Men: Fine. Fine.
Leon: Glad to see you again.
Man: Yeah, bring up a chair.
Leon: Thank you, I will.

Leon: Great bunch of fellows. Ah, my friend, I'm happy to see you again.

Pere: I'm always glad to meet a new customer.
Leon: Um hm.

Pere: And I hope this first visit will not be your last one.

Leon: He's just an old man. His memory is weak.
Ninotchka: What are you after?

Leon: Must one always be after something?
Ninotchka: Your tactics are useless. I'm not Buljanoff, Iranoff or Kopalski.
Leon: Oh, Ninotchka, why must we talk business? If you win the suit, fine. If we win the suit, better. You do me an injustice.

119

Leon: Ninotchka, when we first went to my apartment did I have the slightest idea that you were connected with this deal?

Ninotchka: You know now. And I know now that you're a man who employs business methods which in Russia would be punished by death!

Leon: Oh—death! Death!

Leon: Always so glum!

Leon: What about life, Ninotchka? Do Russians never think about life? Of the moment in which we are living? The only moment we ever really have? Oh, Ninotchka, don't take things so seriously. Nothing's worth it, really. Please—relax. I beg you, Sergeant. Smile.

Ninotchka: What?
Leon: Will you smile?
Ninotchka: Why?
Leon: Oh—well, just smile.
Ninotchka: At what?

Leon: At anything. At the whole ridiculous spectacle of life. At people being so serious. Taking themselves pompously— exaggerating their own importance. If you can't think of anything else to laugh at, you can laugh at you and me.

Ninotchka: Why?

Leon: Because we're an odd couple.
Ninotchka: Then you should go back to your table.
Leon: No. No, I can't leave you. I won't—not yet. Not until I've made you laugh at least once.

Ninotchka: Ha ha.

Ninotchka: Now go back to your table.

Leon: Oh, that's not a laugh. I mean a laugh from the heart.

Leon: I know, I'm going to tell you a funny story. Now wait a minute, let me think of one.

Leon: A—I've got it!

Leon: Well, it seems that there were two Frenchmen who went to America—.

Ninotchka: On which boat?

Leon: On which——

Leon: Oh well, let's drop it. I don't think you'd care very much for that one anyway.
Ninotchka: Probably not.

Leon: Here's a great one.

Leon: Ah—maybe it's not so good. Let's forget it.

Leon: Do you like Scotch stories?
Ninotchka: Never heard one.

Leon: Well here. Two Scotchmen met on the street.

Leon: And I don't know the name of the street. It doesn't matter anyway.

Leon: One's name was McGillicuddy and the other one's name was McIntosh. McGillicuddy said to McIntosh, 'Hello, Mr. McGillicuddy.' And McGillicuddy—McIntosh said to McGillicuddy, 'Hello, Mr. McIn—Mr. McGillicuddy.' Then McGillicuddy said to McIntosh, 'How's Mrs. McIntosh?' And McIntosh said to McGillicuddy, 'How's Mrs. McGillicuddy?'

Ninotchka: I wish they'd never met.

Leon: Yeah, so do I!

Leon: Well, how's this one? Two men are looking at the moon. One of them says to the other, 'Is it true that a lot of people live on the moon?'

Leon: The other one says, 'Sure it's true — about five hundred million.' Then the first one says, 'Whew, they must be pretty crowded when it's half moon!'

Leon: So you don't think that's funny?
Ninotchka: No.
Leon: It seemed funny to me when I first heard it. Maybe the trouble isn't with the joke.

Leon: Maybe it's with you!
Ninotchka: I don't think so.

Leon: I'll give you one more chance. Here goes. When I first heard this joke I laughed myself sick!

Leon: Here goes.

Leon: A man comes into a restaurant. He sits down at the table and he says, 'Waiter, bring me a cup of coffee without cream.' Five minutes later the waiter comes back and says, 'I'm sorry, sir, we have no cream. Can it be without milk?'

Leon: It's good, isn't it? Not funny, huh?
Ninotchka: No.

Leon: Well, it is funny! Everybody else thought it was funny! Maybe you didn't get the point! I'll tell it to you again.

Leon: A man comes into a restaurant.
Leon: Did you get that?
Ninotchka: Yes.
Leon: All right.

Leon: He sits down at the table and he says to the waiter . . . did you get that?
Ninotchka: Yes.

Leon: All right. It isn't funny so far, but wait a minute. He says to the waiter, 'Waiter, bring me a cup of coffee!'

Leon: And five minutes later the waiter comes back and says, 'I'm sorry, sir, we're all out of coffee.'

Leon: Oh, no, no. You've got me all mixed up now.

Leon: Sits down at the table and says, 'Waiter, bring me a cup of coffee.' And five minutes later—that's it.

Leon: He says, 'Waiter bring me a cup of coffee without cream!' And five minutes later the waiter comes back and says, 'I'm sorry, sir, we have no cream. Can it be a glass of milk?'

Leon: Oh, you have no sense of humor!

Leon: None whatsoever. Not a grain of humor in you. There's not a laugh in you. Everybody else laughs at it! But not you!

Leon: What's so funny about this?

Lawyer: In addition to the arguments above enumerated for lifting this injunction,

Lawyer: We wish to cite the decision of the High Court of Paris, rendered in the case of the Princess Marishka

Lawyer: Against the Government of Montenegro on the fifth day of August, eighteen hundred and ninety-seven.

Lawyer: Comparing the facts in that case with our present set of facts, we feel that the Treaty between the Republic of France and USSR —

Ninotchka: I'm sorry, gentlemen.

Ninotchka: The other day I heard such a funny story—it still makes me laugh. It's very funny.

Ninotchka: Oh—yes—about this injunction.
Lawyer: The hearing is set for the twentieth of this month.

Ninotchka: That's two weeks from Thursday.
1st Lawyer: We did our utmost to have it set ahead.

Ninotchka: I know, gentlemen. It's in the hands of the court, we're helpless, aren't we?
Lawyer: Yes, it is unfortunate.

Ninotchka: There's nothing we can do. Why get excited?

1st Lawyer: We'll leave these papers with you for your further consideration. Au revoir, Madame.
Ninotchka: Au revoir.

Lawyer: Au revoir.
Ninotchka: Au revoir.

Ninotchka: Well, that means another two weeks in Paris.
Iranoff: Too bad we have to waste all that time.

Kopalski: I acted on your suggestion, and got in touch with the Power and Light authorities. Whenever you want to visit their plants, they are open to you.
Ninotchka: Oh, yes, Power and Light. Thank you.

Buljanoff: There is something else which I know will appeal to you. A visit to the Paris sewers. They tell me it's extremely instructive.

Ninotchka: Huh? Why don't you get a haircut, Buljanoff?

Ninotchka: You all look so wintry, Comrades.

Ninotchka: And why do we always keep the windows closed?

Ninotchka: Isn't it amazing? At home there is still snow and ice, and here—look at the birds.

Ninotchka: I always felt a little hurt when our swallows deserted us in the winter for capitalistic countries. Now I know why. We have the high ideals, but they have the climate.

Ninotchka: Well, Comrades, I don't think I need you any more.
Iranoff: Is there anything we can do for you?

Ninotchka: No, not a thing. Would you like to go out?
Russians: Yes—yes—sure.

Ninotchka: Have you any money?
Russians: Well—well—

Ninotchka: Here are fifty francs.
Russians: Thank you—oh, thank you.

Ninotchka: Bring me back forty-five.
Iranoff: Yes—
Buljanoff: Of course.
Kopalski: Yes.

Buljanoff: That's fine.
Iranoff: Goodbye, Comrade.

140

Leon: Have you the time, Gaston?
Gaston: It's eight forty-two, sir.
Leon: I guess it must be eight-forty two.

Gaston: You seem to be a bit nervous, sir.
Leon: I am, Gaston.

Gaston: If you'll forgive me, sir. Ever since you met that Bolshevik lady, I've noticed a distinct change in you, sir.
Leon: Have you, Gaston?
Gaston: Decidedly.

Leon: Ah, yes—
Gaston: Yesterday I was greatly amazed when I came from the market and found you'd made your bed, sir.
Leon: Yes—yes, and I felt better for it all day long. I felt as if I'd contributed something.

Gaston: May I add, sir, it was with great amazement that I found a copy of Karl Marx's "Capital" on your night table, sir, That is a socialistic volume which I refuse to so much as dust, sir. I view with alarm, the influence over you of this Bolshevik lady.

Lean: But I don't follow you, Gaston. Isn't it about time that you realized the unfairness of your position? Your being my servant? Wouldn't you like to stand on an equal footing with me?
Gaston: No, sir.

Leon: Good Heavens, isn't there any revolt in you? Sometimes when I order you around, don't you feel like kicking me in the pants?
Gaston: No, sir!

Leon: Oh, you're a reactionary! You can't tell me that you don't look forward to the day when you can come in here, stand square on your two feet and say, "Hey, you, d'Algout, from now on, it's share and share alike!"

Gaston: Emphatically not, sir. The prospect terrifies me. Now, don't misunderstand me, sir. I don't resent your not paying me for the past two months, but the thought that I should split my bank account with you,

Gaston: That you should take half of my life's savings, that is really too much for me, sir.

Leon: Go to bed, little father, go to bed.

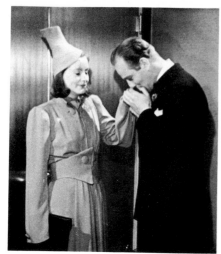

Ninotchka: I don't look too foolish?
Leon: Foolish? If this dress were walking down the Boulevard all by itself, I'd follow it from one end of Paris to the other.

Leon: And when I caught up with it, I'd say, "Wait a moment, you charming little dress. I want you to meet Ninotchka. You two were meant for each other."

Leon: Remember this room?
Ninotchka: I've never been here before.

Ninotchka: I wonder whom you're thinking of.

Ninotchka: Oh, I know. The girl with the map—always figuring out each step, and worrying about North and South.

Leon: Hmm.

Ninotchka: Today—Now, this might shock you. I walked up to a taxi, I said, "Eight-eight-three du Bois." And here I am.
Leon: You see? Life can be so simple.
Ninotchka: For twelve francs, seventy-five.

Leon: Twelve seventy-five? From the Clarence? The son-of-a-gun made a detour.

Leon: But he got you here!

Ninotchka: It's nine o'clock.

Leon: Hmm. That's when one half of Paris says to the other half, "What are your plans for this evening, Madame?"

Ninotchka: First, I would like to take off my hat.

Ninotchka: Then—could we have some music?

Leon: A wonderful idea.

Leon: Radio or records?
Ninotchka: Not radio. Let's have music that's just for ourselves.

Leon: I'll play it very softly, because I have things to tell you about which I can't shout.

Leon: Darling, I—

Leon: You see, I couldn't shout that.

Ninotchka: Oh, Leon!

Ninotchka: Leon, you know the jokes you told me a few days ago? I wake up in the middle of the night and laugh at them.

Ninotchka: You know, that's wrong. They aren't funny—they're silly.

Ninotchka: They're stupid. And still I laugh at them. And when I look at Buljanoff and Iranoff and Kopalski, I know they're scoundrels and I should hate them.

Ninotchka: Then I realize who made them like that, and instead of sending my report to Moscow,

Ninotchka: I go down and buy a ridiculous hat. And if this keeps on—

Ninotchka: Am I too talkative?
Leon: No, no. Go on.

Ninotchka: And, Leon, I want to tell you something which I thought I would never say,

Ninotchka: Which I thought nobody ever should say, because I didn't think it existed. And, Leon — I can't say it.

Leon: What a gesture for a sergeant.

Ninotchka: Leon, may I ask you something?
Leon: Anything.
Ninotchka: If you don't want to answer, you needn't. But if you do, you must tell the truth.
Leon: I promise.

Ninotchka: Did you make any change in this room?
Leon: I don't think so.

Ninotchka: When I was here before I noticed a photograph of a woman on the desk in a wide silver frame. I thought what a waste of silver.

Ninotchka: That's all I was interested in then. Now, I would like to know—what happened to the woman?

Ninotchka: The Grand Duchess?

Ninotchka: She's very attractive. She has great elegance.

Ninotchka: She's what you call a—woman of the world, isn't she?
Leon: Ninotchka. I love you.

Ninotchka: I suppose she's very entertaining. It must be lots of fun to be with a woman like that, so witty and—

Leon: Ninotchka, you're jealous.
Ninotchka: Um-hmm.

Ninotchka: Oh, Leon! Don't ever ask me for a picture of myself. I couldn't bear the thought of being shut up in a drawer.

Ninotchka: I couldn't breathe! I couldn't stand it!
Leon: Oh, my darling!

Headwaiter: Cafe de Lucesse. — A table for tonight? — Certainly, Count d'Algout. What time, may I ask? — After the opera? — Thank you very much.

Headwaiter: Good evening, Your Highness.
Swana: Good Evening, Louis. You seem to be very crowded this evening. Can you manage a table near the floor?
Headwaiter: Certainly, Your Highness, this way please.

Headwaiter: Count d'Algout made the reservations this afternoon.
Swana: Count d'Algout?

Headwaiter: Yes. It is only a small table but we will put in some extra chairs.
Swana: No, no, no, that's another party.

Lady: Why don't we go to some other place? It's so crowded here.
Swana: No, no, no. This is glory. At last I'm going to have a look at that female Bolshevik.

Swana: Can we manage another table?
Headwaiter: Only one in the rear, I'm afraid.
Swana: That's perfect.

2nd Lady: You mean Leon's bringing the Bolshevik you told us about?
Swana: Isn't it divine?
Lady: I wouldn't have missed this for anything in the world.

Swana: Now, we must be very discreet. If she sucks her soup and drinks out of her finger bowl, I don't want anybody to laugh.

Swana: We mustn't embarrass poor little Leon. He's gone through enough for my sake. We mustn't add insult to injury.

Headwaiter: Is this satisfactory, Your Highness?

Headwaiter: Is it to be dinner, Your Excellency?
General: Oh, later, perhaps. We'll just start with champagne.

161

Headwaiter: Champagne.

Swana: I'm only afraid the doorman may spoil all our fun. If only he lets her in.

Man: Look, there's Leon.
Swana: Where?

Waiter: Good evening, Count d'Algout.
Leon: Good evening.
Waiter: If you please.

Swana: General, shall we dance?

Leon: Is it dry?
Waiter: Yes, Monsieur.

Leon: Is that right, or do you prefer it sweet?

Ninotchka: Oh, I wouldn't know. The closest I ever came to champagne was in a newsreel. The wife of some president was throwing it at a battleship.

Leon: It's always good luck to launch something with champagne —a battleship—or an evening.

Ninotchka: It's funny to look back. I was brought up on goat's milk. I had a ration of vodka in the army—and now champagne.

Leon: From goats to grapes. That's drinking in the right direction.

Ninotchka: It's good.
Leon: Um hm.

Ninotchka: From what I've read, I thought champagne was a strong drink—it's delicate. Does anyone ever get drunk on this?

Leon: Mmm, well, there have been cases.

Leon: But the headache the next morning is worthwhile if you drink it with the right toast.

Leon: To us, Ninotchka.

Swana: Thank you, General.

Swana: Hello, Leon! How are you, my dear!
Leon: Hello, Swana.

Leon: Good evening, General.
General: How do you do.

Swana: My, you're looking magnificent tonight, isn't he, General?
General: Yes.
Leon: Thank you.

Swana: Is this your new dress suit?
Leon: Yes, Swana.
Swana: Didn't I tell you Benson and Benson were the tailors for you?
Leon: Yes, Swana, you did.
Swana: It's a dream of beauty. He never takes my word for anything. But I was right, wasn't I?
Leon: Yes, Swana.

Swana: Oh, am I interrupting?
Leon: No—no, not at all. Your Highness, may I present Comrade Yakushova?
Swana: How do you do?
Ninotchka: How do you do?
Leon: General Savitzky.
General: How do you do?
Ninotchka: How do you do?

Swana: Oh, I've some wonderful news for you, Leon. It's about Punchy. Do you mind if I sit down?
Leon: No, no, please.

Swana: General, would you mind making my excuses at our table?
General: Certainly.
Swana: Will you say I'll be back in a few moments?

Swana: Well, Leon, we can be proud of our . . .

Swana: Punchy. He had a triumph at the Dog Show. He won another blue ribbon and bit the judge. I bought him the loveliest little sweater as a reward.

Swana: You should see him strutting down the street in it. He looks like a little boulevardien. You see, Count d'Algout gave me Punchy for my birthday. You must have searched for weeks before you found anything as divine as Punchy, didn't you, Leon?

Leon: Months, Swana.
Swana: Oh, poor Madame Yakushova—here we are talking in mysteries. I'm sure you wonder what it's all about.

Ninotchka: Not at all. I understand perfectly. Count d'Algout gave **you** a dog. You made it very clear, Madame.

Swana: Oh, dear me. I must be losing my finesse. If I'm not careful I'll be understood by everybody.

Leon: Charming crowd here tonight, isn't there?
Swana: Well, I'm going, Leon, **but** before I go, I must compliment you on your gown, Madame Yakushova.

Swana: Is that what they're wearing in Moscow this year?

Ninotchka: No—last year, Madame.

Swana: Isn't it amazing. One gets the wrong impression of the new Russia. It must be charming.

Swana: I'm delighted conditions have improved so. I assume this is what the factory workers wear at their dances?
Ninotchka: Exactly.

Ninotchka: You see, it would have been very embarrassing for people of my sort to wear low cut gowns in the old Russia. The lashes of the Cossacks across our backs were not very becoming, and you know how vain women are.

Swana: Yes, you're quite right about the Cossacks. We made a great mistake when we let them use their whips. They had such reliable guns.

Leon: Will you do me a favor? Let's not talk about the good old days.

Swana: Yes, it's a very wise suggestion, Leon. I'm afraid Madame and I will never agree. The only thing we have in common is our lawsuit and that will be settled next week.

Swana: I understand everything will be over by Thursday. Am I right?

Ninotchka: Yes. You're right, Madame. It'll all be over by Thursday.

Swana: It's too bad you have so few more days here in Paris.

Swana: Now Leon, be sure and redouble your efforts so that Madame can take some pleasant memories when she returns to Moscow. Good night. Good night, Leon.
Leon: Good night, Swana.

Ninotchka: Now I think I need a glass of champagne.

Ninotchka: Quickly, please, tell me one of your funny stories.

Leon: A funny story?
Ninotchka: Um hm. You never finished the one about the a— about the two Scotchmen with the names.
Leon: Oh.
Ninotchka: Please.

Leon: Well, there were two Scotchmen.
Ninotchka: Uh huh.
Leon: One's name was McIntosh and the other one was McGillicuddy.
Ninotchka: Uh huh.
Leon: They met on the street.
Ninotchka: Hmm.

Leon: No, I'll tell you another story. A much better one. The only thing that'll be over on Thursday will be the lawsuit.

Leon: There'll be no Thursday for us. Next week or any other week. I won't let it happen. I'll tear it out of the calendar. Isn't that a good story?

Ninotchka: Wonderful—if one can believe it.

Leon: You must, darling.

Ninotchka: To the loveliest story I ever heard.

Ninotchka: Let's dance.

174

Ninotchka: Oh, Leon, something is the matter.

Leon: Oh, you just made that trip from goats to grapes a little too quickly.
Ninotchka: Everything is so wonderful. It's getting farther and farther away.
Leon: What, darling?

Ninotchka: Thursday.
Leon: Yes, don't worry, everything's going to be all right.

Ninotchka: Comrades! Comrades!

Leon: Darling, darling, please.
Ninotchka: I want to talk to my brothers.
Leon: Shhh.

Ninotchka: Don't shush me, please. I am the people. I want to hold a speech. I want to overthrow the Grand Duchess.
Leon: Ninotchka, you can't do that.
Ninotchka: Oh, Comrades! The good people of France!
Leon: Now, now, now, Ninotchka.

Ninotchka: Oh, but they're all Grand Duchesses here.

Ninotchka: I ordered out thousands of Grand Duchesses and I want to tell them——.
Leon: Yes, dear. Yes, dear, you're quite right.
Ninotchka: Yes, I——.

Leon: But first of all, you're going through that door. You're going to lie down and take some spirits of ammonia.

Ninotchka: Oh, no speech?
Leon: No speech.
Ninotchka: Oh—I love you, my little Leonitchka.
Leon: And I adore you, Ninotchka.

Leon: Go ahead, now.

Ninotchka: No speech?

Leon: No! No! For heaven's sake, no speech!
Ninotchka: No speech.

Leon: Give me a double brandy.
Bartender: Yes, sir.

Manager: I'm very sorry, Count D'Algout.

Manager: It is most embarrassing, but the lady you brought with you tonight is spreading Communistic propaganda in the Powder Room.

Leon: What? Give me another double brandy.

Manager: That kind of propaganda is bad anywhere, but inciting the attendants of the Powder Room to go on strike! Well, if she succeeds, the consequences will be disastrous.

Leon: Well, what can I do about it?

Manager: She has been asked to leave the Powder Room, but without success. We would appreciate it very much if you would see to it yourself.

Leon: Yeah. You want me to go in there?
Manager: I'm sorry, sir, but I must insist.

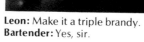

Leon: Make it a triple brandy.
Bartender: Yes, sir.

Leon: All right, tell the Grand Duchess! Tell everybody! They know it anyway. It doesn't make any difference.

Leon: Go on, get out. Get out! Get out!

Ninotchka: Don't tell them where we're going.
Leon: No, Darling, nobody will find us.

Ninotchka: Are we going to build our little house?
Leon: Yes, a little white house.

Ninotchka: No, not white.
Leon: All right, we'll make it red.
Ninotchka: No, let's not have any color. No color. Just a house house. Let's form our own party.

Leon: Right. Lovers of the world, unite.

Ninotchka: And we won't stretch up our arms.
Leon: No! No! No!

Ninotchka: And we won't clench our fist.
Leon: No! No!

Ninotchka: Our salute will be a kiss.
Leon: Yes, a kiss. Salute!

Ninotchka: I am so happy.

Ninotchka: Oh, I'm so happy!

Ninotchka: No one can be so happy without being punished. I will be punished and I should be punished. Leon, I want to confess.
Leon: I know. It's the Russian soul.

Ninotchka: Well, everyone wants to confess. And if they don't confess, they make them confess. I am a traitor. When I kissed you, I betrayed the Russian ideal. I should be stood up against the wall.

Leon: Would that make you any happier?
Ninotchka: Much happier.
Leon: All right.

Ninotchka: I've paid the penalty. Now, let's have some music.

Leon: Yes, let's turn on the radio.
Ninotchka: Radio? What's radio?
Leon: Radio's a little box that you buy on the installment plan and before you tune it in, they tell you there's a new model out.

Ninotchka: Oh, yes, I know where that is.

Ninotchka: There's one around here somewhere. It has a . . . it has a little knob which you turn.
Leon: A little knob, that's right.

Ninotchka: Yeah. Maybe it's in here.
Leon: Just a little knob.

Ninotchka: It's a radio and has a knob. Now, maybe it's in here.
Leon: Just a little knob.
Ninotchka: Let's see.

Ninotchka: There it is. There's the

Ninotchka: knob.

Leon: There's the knob.

Leon: Now, what shall we get, the news?

Ninotchka: No news. We don't want to know what's happening in the world. We want to be left alone, don't we?
Leon: Yes, Darling, all by ourselves.

Ninotchka: Then turn to the . . . the left and stop at seven.
Leon: Turn to the left and stop at seven.

Ninotchka: No music.
Leon: No, no music.

Ninotchka: There it is, Thursday.

Ninotchka: You can't rip it out of the week.

Ninotchka: There they are. They're terrible things, those jewels.

Leon: Oh, but big!

Ninotchka: They are the tears of Old
Russia. See that stone?
Leon: Who cried that one?

Ninotchka: Czar Peter gave it to his wife,
Catherine the Great.

Ninotchka: For it he sold ten thousand
serfs in the market.

Leon: Oh, but Darling, don't get impatient.

Leon: Wait till we're married. You know
that worthless butler of mine, that
reactionary? Some day I'll come home to
you and I'll say,

Leon: "Darling, I drove Gaston to the market this morning and oh,
look what I got for him!"

Leon: Darling, come here.

Leon: Let me put this on you.

Ninotchka: No, no, no!
Leon: Yes.
Ninotchka: No, no!

Leon: You will teach these jewels. For the first time they will learn how they can really look.
Ninotchka: They belong to the people.

Leon: And I give them back to the people.

Leon: I make you Ninotchka the Great, Duchess of the People, Grand Duchess of the People.

Ninotchka: Is this the wish of the masses?

Leon: It is their wish.
Ninotchka: Thank you, Leon.

Ninotchka: Thank you, masses.

Ninotchka: Can I make a speech now?
Leon: Please.

Ninotchka: Comrades! People of the world! The revolution is on the march. I know.

Ninotchka: Bombs will fall, civilization will crumble.

Ninotchka: But not yet, please.

Ninotchka: Wait. What's the hurry? Give us our moment.

Ninotchka: Let's be happy.

Ninotchka: We're happy, aren't we, Leon?
Leon: Yes, Darling.

Ninotchka: So happy . . . and so tired. Oh!

  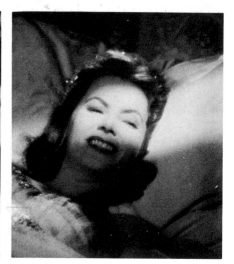

Ninotchka: Smile, Little Father. Smile!

Ninotchka: Come in.

Swana: Good morning.
Ninotchka: What?

Swana: It's tomorrow morning—tomorrow noon, to be exact. I hope you will forgive me. I know it's extremely cruel to awaken anyone at such an hour. Don't you recognize me? I'm the Grand Duchess Swana.

Swana: Yes, I know exactly how you feel, my dear. The morning after always does look grim if you happen to be wearing last night's dress.

Swana: Don't be embarrassed by my presence, though. You couldn't have found anyone more sympathetic to your condition.

Ninotchka: I think we can cut your visit short. Leon is not here.

Swana: Of course not, my dear. I didn't come here with any such suspicion. How ridiculous! Nor did I come here to pick up his hat.

Ninotchka: What is it you people always say, regardless of what you mean: "I am delighted to have you here?" I haven't reached that state of civilization, therefore I must ask you to leave.

Swana: Leave? That's exactly what I came here to ask you to do. Leave.
Swana: I don't mean this hotel and I don't mean Paris—I mean France. There's a plane for Moscow at five-forty.

Ninotchka: Do you still think you're issuing orders from your palace in Petrograd?

Swana: My palace in Petrograd. Yes, you took that away from me. You took away my Czar, my country, my people. Everything I had. But nothing more!

Ninotchka: People cannot be taken away, madame, neither a hundred and sixty million nor one. Not if you have their love. You hadn't. That's why you're not in Russia any longer, and that's why you came here this morning.

Ninotchka: Problems were never solved by bowing from a balcony.
Swana: Oh, my dear, you don't know how impressive I could be.

Swana: Did you ever see me in my ragalia with my diadem and all my jewels?

Ninotchka: Elysee 2763.

Swana: Believe me, Leon can't help you. He doesn't know anything about the jewels.

Swana: I give you my word. I swear it.

196

Ninotchka: Where are they?
Swana: You were very careless with our precious jewels, my dear. They're too expensive a toy for two children to play with.

Ninotchka: Where are they?
Swana: Now don't worry. Fortunately, last night a very trustworthy friend kept his eyes open.

Swana: He may have overstepped his function as a waiter, but he fulfilled his duty as a Russian.

Swana: I just put this on for sentiment.

Swana: The rest are absolutely safe, I assure you. But, if you feel like notifying the police—.

Ninotchka: You leave me no choice.
Swana: Won't it be rather embarrassing for a Soviet Envoy to disclose the circumstances under which she lost them?

Ninotchka: I'll have to face the consequences but so will you. Don't forget, they'll ask you how you got them.

Swana: That's very simple to answer. They were given to me by my mother, they were given to her by her mother, in fact, they're mine. You can't steal what belongs to you.

Ninotchka: They always belonged to the Russian people. They paid for them with their blood, their lives, and you'll give them back.

Swana: I told you we had plenty to talk about. Shall we sit down?

Swana: Now let's free ourselves from emotionalism and try to solve the problem in a practical way.

Swana: Our situation has considerably changed. Before I had only a claim to the jewels. Now I have the jewels.

Ninotchka: In other words, moral ideas have no weight with you. All right, then let's deal with legal facts. You know that France has recognized the Soviet.

Swana: Unfortunately.

Ninotchka: Under the Soviet law the jewels belong to the state. France is going to uphold that ownership.

Swana: Yes, my lawyer agrees with you. He says that France will uphold it in every court, but, I will drag you through every court, don't forget that. And when I say it will take two years I am, as always, conservative.

Ninotchka: Won't those two years in court be expensive for you? I know that money was no object as long as you could squeeze it out of the pockets of the people but now —

Swana: I may run out of money, but you have already run out of bread.

Swana: Two years is a long time for your comrades to wait.

Ninotchka: I see. You've calculated it in terms of hunger.
Swana: No, I just wanted to be absolutely impartial. Both of us are faced with two rather uncomfortable years.
Swana: We can condense those two years to two minutes if you want to accept my proposition.
Ninotchka: Go on.

Swana: I am willing to hand over the jewels and sign any necessary papers if you will take that five-forty plane to Moscow.
Ninotchka: That's not the way to win him back—not Leon.

Swana: I think I know Leon quite as well as you—perhaps a little better. Leave that worry to me.

Swana: Now, five-forty leaves you time enough to close the deal with Monsieur Mercier—but, a—naturally you'll be too busy for any farewells.

Swana: I will see to it that everything is done in the most expeditious manner. And I will also see you to the airport.

Swana: That's my proposition, Comrade Yakushova.

Ninotchka: Yes? Oh, hello.

Ninotchka: Yes, Leon. No—you didn't waken me.

Ninotchka: I'm fine, thank you. Yes—oh, yes, it was wonderful.

Ninotchka: For luncheon?

Ninotchka: I'm afraid I can't. I have lots of things to attend to today, Leon.

Ninotchka: I'm going to be very busy.

Ninotchka: Well, to tell you the truth, I'm a little tired and I would like to rest. — Maybe you're right. Perhaps it is the champagne.

Ninotchka: For dinner? Of course. — Seven o'clock here. Seven o'clock will be all right.

Ninotchka: Yes. Just a moment.

Ninotchka: Come in.

Ninotchka: You can leave it here.
Bellboy: Yes, Madame.

and Sweetheart, I have kept my first promise. I sent poor old Gaston to the market this morning and if you will look deep into the flowers you will see what I got for him.

Ninotchka: Operator, will you switch the call, please?

Ninotchka: Darling, your present just arrived. It's very silly . . . and very wonderful.

Ninotchka: What?—I won't forget. Seven o'clock. Goodbye, darling.—What?—Oh, salute.

Swana: Good afternoon, Jacqueline.
Maid: Good afternoon, Your Highness. Madame, I . . . I . . . .

Swana: Yes, I know. You didn't find my other glove. Well, it's all right. You're forgiven.
Maid: Thank you, Your Highness.

Maid: Count D'Algout is waiting. He's been here some time.
Swana: Oh, Count D'Algout? Here.

Swana: Oh, Leon, darling! How nice! Have you ordered tea or a cocktail?
Leon: No, thanks, Swana.

Swana: Did I act stupidly last night? Should I apologize?

Leon: No. I'm the one that should apologize. I should have talked to you before.

Swana: Is this, by any chance, going to be a confession?
Leon: Yes.

Swana: Oh, no, no, no, no, my little Volga Boatman. Have you forgotten our First Commandment? Never Complain, Never Explain.

Swana: Now, it's worked so often and so perfectly in the past, let's not break the rule. And, please, don't look so guilty. Otherwise, I'll . . .

Leon: Swana, just this once. I must ask you to listen to me.

Swana: All right. I'm listening.

Leon: I know you hate the obvious, but do you mind if, for the moment, I'm not the least subtle?
Swana: Brutal frankness, if you insist.
Leon: There are a hundred ways of approaching it, but I feel it can best be said in one simple phrase. I'm in love, Swana.

Swana: Oh, I thought it was something serious! How could you frighten me so?
Leon: It must be serious.

Leon: Not so long ago I'd have considered such a statement juvenile and rather middle class. Now I can say it without a stammer, without a blush. I'm in love, Swana.

Swana: But, Leon, this has the ugly sound of regeneration!
Leon: I'm afraid that's what it is, Swana.

Swana: Always late. Same old trouble, Leon.

Swana: Whether you're taking me to the opera, or calling for me at a beauty shop, you're never on time. And now, when it's a question of your reform, late again—

Swana: By about five minutes.

Leon: What is this, Swana?
Swana: Well, knowing the efficiency of the French Air Service, I think I can safely guarantee that Madame Yakushova has already taken off for Moscow.

Leon: Has done what?
Swana: She's gone, Leon.
Leon: You don't expect me to believe that?

Swana: There's the telephone.

Swana: If you call the hotel, you'll find you have no seven o'clock appointment.

Buljanoff: Imagine. For once in our lives we were in Paris and we never went to the Eiffel Tower.
Kopalski: That's right.
Iranoff: They tell me it has a wonderful restaurant on the second floor.

Ninotchka: Yes, it is an amazing piece of engineering, still the most remarkable iron structure in the world. Hmm.

Ninotchka: Leading to the top there is a staircase of over a thousand steps.

Ninotchka: But there is an elevator included in the price of admission.

Clerk: Well, everything is in order. I hope you will enjoy your trip to Russia, Madame.

Woman: Thank you. Oh, by the way, I've heard so many rumors about laundry conditions in Russia. Is it advisable to take one's own towels?

Clerk: Certainly not, Madame. That is only capitalistic propaganda. We change the towel every week.
Woman: Oh, thank you.

Clerk: Hello. — Comrade Cazabine? No, I am sorry. He hasn't been with us for six months. He was called back to Russia and was investigated.

Clerk: You can get further details from his widow. — You're very welcome, very welcome.

Leon: Pardon me. I . . . I was interested in what you were just saying.

Leon: Do you mean when an envoy goes back to Russia and they don't like what he's done, they put him out of the way?

Clerk: Not always. Look at me. I've been back twice.

Leon: Here's my passport. Please give me a visa. I must leave for Russia immediately.
Clerk: Count Leon D'Algout. A count! A nobleman!

Leon: Don't hold that against me, please.

Clerk: Why should an aristocrat want to go to Russia?
Leon: Business.
Clerk: What business?
Leon: Private.

Clerk: There is no private business in Russia. This whole things seems very suspicious. What is the real reason? If you ever want to get into Russia, take my advice. Confess!

Leon: Listen. I'll be absolutely frank with you. I have no business in Moscow.
Clerk: I think so, too.

Leon: I want to see a friend of mine, a very dear friend. It's a personal matter that has no relation to social philosophies or politics. It's a girl.

Clerk: So, it is love which drags you to Moscow!
Leon: Yes.

Clerk: No visa.

Leon: But I must get into that country of yours!
Clerk: Oh no, no visa.
Leon: But that's impossible! You can't do it!

Leon: You haven't the right to . . . Listen. If you don't give me that visa . . . !
Clerk: You're going to force us, huh?

Leon: Look here! You advertise all over the world for people to go into your country

Leon: And then when somebody tries to get in, you won't let them!
Clerk: Why should I take a chance?
Leon: On what?

Clerk: How do I know you don't want to blow up a factory?
Leon: What for? Why?
Clerk: Or a tunnel, or a bridge?

Leon: Oh, suspicions! Nothing but suspicions! That's the trouble with you.

Leon: Listen! If you don't let me in, I'll stand in front of this office of yours and warn people to keep away from Russia! I'll picket your whole country!

Leon: I'll boycott you, that's what I'll do! No more vodka, no more caviar,

Leon: No more Tchaikovsky!

Leon: No more borscht!

213

Leon: Oh, wait a minute. I've got a better idea than that.
Clerk: What?

Leon: And you can tell the Kremlin that's just the beginning!

Clerk: No visa.

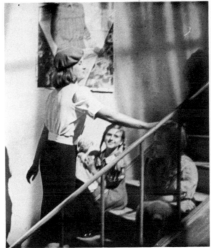

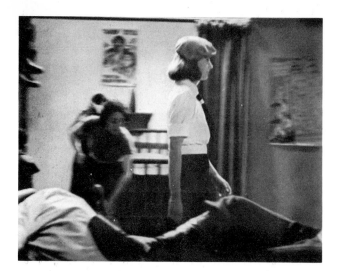

Ninotchka: Good afternoon, Anna.
Anna: Oh, good afternoon, Ninotchka.

Ninotchka: Aren't you late?

Anna: No. The opera starts an hour later tonight, on account of the parade.
Ninotchka: Didn't you march today?
Anna: They didn't let me.

Anna: I'm in disgrace. Last week, at the performance of "Carmen," I played a sour note. The conductor got so excited, he yelled, "There is sabotage in the string section!"

Ninotchka: Too bad, Anna. You missed an inspiring day.
Anna: Yes, I know.

Anna: Are you expecting someone?

Ninotchka: A few friends. Just a small dinner party.
Anna: And what are you serving?
Ninotchka: An omelet.

Anna: An omelet? Aren't you living a little above your ration?
Ninotchka: I've saved two eggs and each of my friends is bringing his own. We'll manage.

Anna: Just goes to prove the theory of our State.

Anna: If you stand alone, it means a boiled egg, but if you're true to the collective spirit and stick together, you've got an omelet.

Anna: That reminds me. Have you heard the latest they're telling about the Kremlin? Well, one man . . .

Anna: I'll tell you later.

Anna: Ah, that Gurganov! You never know whether he's on his way to the washroom, or the Secret Police.
Ninotchka: You should be more careful, Anna.

Anna: And you, too, Ninotchka.
Ninotchka: About what?

Anna: Oh, ever since you have been back from Paris, I . . .
Ninotchka: I haven't talked to anyone about Paris. I haven't said a word.

Anna: That's just it. It makes people feel queer. And I don't want you to get in any trouble.
Ninotchka: I have nothing to hide.

Anna: You should. I'll show you.

Anna: When I passed through the laundry yard today, I saw all the women huddled around this, so I brought it up here.

Anna: Things like this create a bad feeling. First they didn't know whose it was . . . and then they saw the Paris label and did it start a commotion!

Anna: Some said it's what we all ought to wear. Others said it's like hanging foreign ideas on our clothesline. It undermines our whole cause.

Ninotchka: I see.

Anna: You know how it is today. All you have to do is wear a pair of silk stockings and they suspect you of counter revolution.

Ninotchka: Thank you, Anna. I'll dry it up here when I wash it next. I should hate to see our country endangered by my underwear.

Anna: Ninotchka, I'm your friend. You can trust me. Did you bring back anything else?

Ninotchka: No. I left everything in Paris. I just happened to be wearing this.
Anna: Tell me, what else did you have?
Ninotchka: Well, a hat.

Anna: What was it like?
Ninotchka: Oh, it was very silly. I'd be ashamed to wear it here.

Anna: As beautiful as that! What else? Come, tell me.

Ninotchka: An evening gown.
Anna: An evening gown?

Ninotchka: Yes. It's a dress you wear in the evening.
Anna: What do you wear in the morning?

Ninotchka: When you get up you wear a negligee, then you change into a morning frock.

Anna: You mean to tell me you wear a different dress for different times of the day?
Ninotchka: Yes.

Anna: Now, Ninotchka, you are exaggerating!

Ninotchka: No, it's true. That's how they live in the other world. Here we dress to cover up our bodies . . . to keep warm.
Anna: And there?

Ninotchka: Sometimes they're not completely covered, but . . . a . . . they don't freeze.

Anna: Oh, they must have wonderful materials to make a thing like this. So soft! Something you don't even see.
Ninotchka: You feel it, though.

Anna: Ninotchka, I . . . I wouldn't bring this up if we weren't such good friends.

Ninotchka: What is it, Anna?
Anna: You know I . . . I told you that Pavlov and I are going to get married when he comes back from the maneuvers.

Anna: Would it be asking too much if . . . ?
Ninotchka: You want this?
Anna: Just for the honeymoon.

Ninotchka: It's yours for good. It's my . . . **Anna:** Ninotchka! Ninotchka!

Anna: Thank you. Thank you very much. **Anna:** I'll never, never forget what you've done.

Anna: Am I going to play that cadenza tonight!

Radio voice: Individuals?

Radio voice: Yes! As atoms in the cosmos of Soviet Russia!

Another radio voice: And thirty million peasants, eighty-five per cent of the population!

Another radio voice: . . . into an automobile and the Muzhik into a tractor, and then let the Capitalists try to keep . . .

Ninotchka: No music.

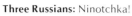

Iranoff: Ninotchka.

Buljanoff: Ninotchka.

Three Russians: Ninotchka!

Ninotchka: Buljanoff, Iranoff and Kopalski.

Ninotchka: How are you, you three scoundrels!

Kopalski: Well, we are back home.
Buljanoff: You know what they say—there is nothing like home.

Iranoff: Yes, and we might as well face it.

Ninotchka: Now you mustn't talk that way, you must adjust yourselves.

Ninotchka: Let's be brave.

Iranoff: Brave—that's right.
Ninotchka: Come and sit down.

Buljanoff: Let's be happy that we are all alive.

Iranoff: And that's something we owe to Ninotchka. If you hadn't given Commissar Razinin such a wonderful report about us, who knows what would have happened?

Buljanoff: I can tell you exactly.

Ninotchka: Comrades, let's forget everything except we're together.

Iranoff: Yes, let's do that!
Kopalski: It's a real Paris reunion.

Iranoff: If you close your eyes and listen to our voices, we might be in Paris.

Ninotchka: Let's not close our eyes. There are many good things to see here, too.

Kopalski: Look how nicely she has arranged the table.

Iranoff: Yes, how lovely. And what a wonderful room you have here.

Buljanoff: How many families live here with you?
Ninotchka: Only myself and two other girls. One is a cello player in the opera and the other is a street-car conductor.

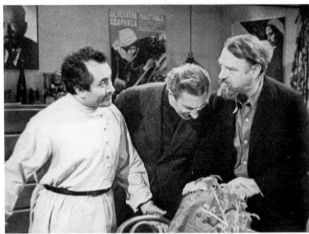

Iranoff: Just three people in a room this size? Oh—
Buljanoff: And your own radio. Look here—isn't that wonderful?
Iranoff: Look at this—what good material.
Kopalski: Naturally, it's not the Royal Suite.

Ninotchka: Comrades, once and for all, we are in Moscow.

Kopalski: Yes, there's no doubt of that. Just look out of the window and there it is.

Ninotchka: And it's great! Think what it was a few years ago and what it is now.

Ninotchka: It's a tremendous achievement.

Ninotchka: You must be reasonable, Comrades.

Iranoff: She is right. Anyhow, let's talk ourselves into it.

Buljanoff: All right. It's great! It's marvelous. It's wonderful!

Buljanoff: Just see how happy the people look—from here.
Kopalski: Can you blame them? At least the May Day Parade is over.
Buljanoff: That's another thing—it's spring.

Ninotchka: The same spring we had in Paris. Just as good.

Kopalski: Even the swallows are back.

Iranoff: Really? Yes, that's right. Maybe it's the same swallow we saw in Paris.

Buljanoff: Um—yes, it is, Ninotchka. It is. He must have been in Paris. You can see it in his whole attitude. He just picked up a crumb of our black bread—shook his head and dropped it.

Ninotchka: We must be patient. Finally we got the spring, didn't we?

Iranoff: Oh, let's forget the future. Let's stop being sentimental. Let's start that omelet.
Kopalski: That's right.
Buljanoff: Oh, yes—a om—

Kopalski: Here is my egg.
Iranoff: And here is mine.
Ninotchka: And here are mine.

Buljanoff: I don't know—where's my egg?

Buljanoff: I had an egg, too.

Buljanoff: Comrades, I am out of the omelet.

 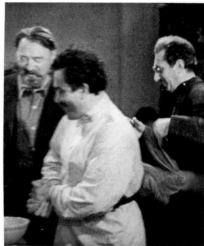 

Ninotchka: Don't worry, there'll be enough.
Iranoff: Of course—come on!

Buljanoff: Thank you.
Iranoff: Now come over here.
Kopalski: Buljanoff—come on.

Iranoff: Come, Ninotchka, let's make it in real Parisian style.
Ninotchka: Yeah.

Kopalski: Let's fill it with confitures, des prunes.

Iranoff: A man like that. All he has to do is walk through a room and the omelet drops.
Ninotchka: Yeah.
Buljanoff: Yes.

All sing: *Paris!*
I still adore you.

Buljanoff: *Adore you—ha ha.*

All: *Paris, I'm longing for you.*

Buljanoff: *For you, for you, Paris.*

All: *You know—Left my heart in your—*

All: *For you . . . —*

Vladimir: Comrade Yakushova, here, the postman left this letter for you.

Ninotchka: Thank you, Vladimir.

Iranoff: What is it, Ninotchka?
Kopalski: Ninotchka, what is it?
Ninotchka: It's from Paris.

Buljanoff: From Paris?
Kopalski: A bill?
Ninotchka: From Leon.
Iranoff: From Leon? How is he—tell us—how is he?

236

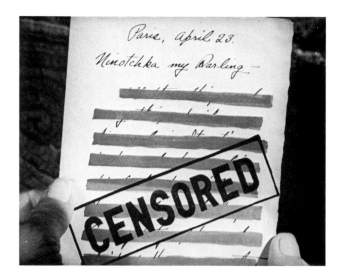

Iranoff: Bad news?

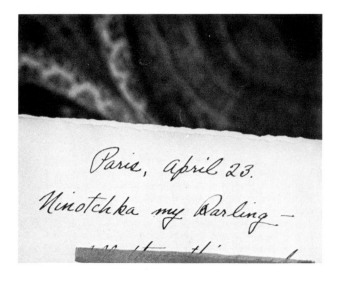

Kopalski: Well, I think it´s getting late.

Iranoff: Good night, Ninotchka.
Ninotchka: Good night.
Iranoff: Thanks, for a wonderful dinner.

Kopalski: Good night, Ninotchka.
Ninotchka: Good night.

Buljanoff: Good night.

Buljanoff: They can't censor our memories, can they?
Ninotchka: No.

Razinin: Come in.

Razinin: Good morning, Comrade.

Ninotchka: Good morning, Comrade Commissar. Here is my report on the materials available for trading in next four months.
Razinin: Does it include the products of the far eastern provinces?
Ninotchka: Yes, it does.

Razinin: You mean you have finished the whole investigation?
Ninotchka: Yes.
Razinin: That's marvelous. You must have worked day and night. Don't you ever sleep?
Ninotchka: I need very little sleep. We must be extremely careful what goods we take in exchange. I have already started a survey on our most urgent needs.

Razinin: Well, Comrade, I am afraid you will have to turn over that work to someone else.
Ninotchka: May I ask why?

Razinin: Please sit down.
Ninotchka: Thank you.

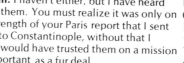

Razinin: Now, Comrade have you heard from your friends, Kopalski, Buljanoff and Iranoff?
Ninotchka: No.

Razinin: I haven't either, but I have heard about them. You must realize it was only on the strength of your Paris report that I sent them to Constantinople, without that I never would have trusted them on a mission as important as a fur deal.
Ninotchka: May I ask what has happened?

Razinin: If I told you what's going on in Constantinople right now, you wouldn't believe it. They are sitting there those three, for six weeks and haven't sold a piece of fur. This anonymous report was sent me. They are dragging the good name of our country through every cafe and night club. Here—

Razinin: "How can the Bolshevik cause gain respect among the Moslems if your three representatives, Buljanoff, Iranoff and Kopalski get so drunk that they threw a carpet out of their hotel window and complain to the management that it didn't fly!" Unbelievable! It's an outrage!

Ninotchka: They shouldn't do such things. Are you sure this report's correct?

Razinin: Naturally, I want to verify it, and that's why I need you.
Ninotchka: You want me to go to Constantinople?
Razinin: Yes—leaving immediately.

Ninotchka: I appreciate your confidence in me, but I must ask you to entrust someone else with this mission. I should hate to interrupt my present work.

Ninotchka: I am positive my survey is more important than finding out whether three of our Comrades have been drinking some extra glasses of champagne.

Razinin: That is for me to decide, Comrade Yakushova!

Ninotchka: I am sorry. I don't want to overstep my position, but . . . uh . . . please, don't send me.

Ninotchka: Please, Comrade, let me stay here. Let me finish my work. I'm in the rhythm of it now. I don't want to go away.

Ninotchka: I don't want to be sent into that foreign atmosphere again. It throws you out of gear. Let me finish my work. I have concentrated everything in it.

Ninotchka: Please, don't make me go.

243

Razinin: Don't waste my time, Comrade. Do your duty. Goodbye.

Ninotchka: I shall do my best.

Kopalski: How do you like it, Ninotchka? Isn't it wonderful?
Iranoff: Tell us, Ninotchka!
Buljanoff: Tell us, Ninotchka!

Ninotchka: Buljanoff, Iranoff—Kopalski—

Iranoff: Now, please Ninotchka—don't start figuring it out in cows.
Buljanoff: Ahhh!

Ninotchka: You've done it again and I am responsible. How can you forget yourselves this way? You were sent here to make money not to spend it.

Iranoff: Buljanoff—she still has those old fashioned ideas.
Buljanoff: Uh-huh. It is high time she got out of Russia.
Kopalski: Yes.

Ninotchka: Comrades! I must be stern with you.

Kopalski: That's our old Ninotchka.
Iranoff: Yes.
Buljanoff: Yes.

Ninotchka: Don't forget the day will come when you will have to face Razinin.

Buljanoff: Razinin? Good old Razinin.

Buljanoff: Is he still alive? How does he manage?

Ninotchka: Comrades—

Kopalski: Friends, Ninotchka—we are friends.

Buljanoff: Imagine—we don't have to whisper any more.
Iranoff: No! We can say whatever we want.

Iranoff: We can shout—we can complain. Look!

Iranoff: The service in this hotel is terrible!

Iranoff: See? Nobody comes.

Iranoff: Nobody pays any attention.

Iranoff: That's freedom.
Buljanoff: That's bad management.

Ninotchka: Is it possible to bring you back to reality for a moment. I must have a complete report of your negotiations and a detailed expense account.

Buljanoff: No, no, Ninotchka—don't ask for it. There is a Turkish proverb which says 'If something smells bad, why put your nose in it?'

Ninotchka: And there is an old Russian saying 'The cat who has cream on his whiskers had better find good excuses.'

Buljanoff: With our cream situation as it is, it's Russia that should apologize to the cats.

Ninotchka: Well, I don't know how I can get you out of it this time.

Ninotchka: How will it end.

Buljanoff: Shall we tell her?
Kopalski: Yes.
Iranoff: Yes.

Buljanoff: Ninotchka, I hope you'll be our guest.
Ninotchka: Guest?
Buljanoff: Yes, we have opened a restaurant.
Ninotchka: A restaurant?

Iranoff: We have a wonderful electric sign "Dine with Buljanoff, Iranoff and Kopalski."

Ninotchka: You mean you're deserting Russia?
Iranoff: Hmm!

Kopalski: Oh, Ninotchka, don't call it desertion. Our little restaurant—that is our Russia. The Russia of borscht, the Russia of boeuf strogonoff, of blinis and sour cream.
Iranoff: The Russia of piroshka . . . people will eat and love it.

Buljanoff: Ah, and we are not only serving good food, we are serving our country. We are making friends.

Ninotchka: Who gave you this idea? Who's responsible for all this?

Iranoff, Buljanoff and Kopalski: Oh, ahh!

Kopalski: There is something in Constantinople—something irresistible.

Iranoff: It's in the air. It may come around the corner when you walk down the street.

Buljanoff: It may step out of a bazaar. It may be waiting for you in a corridor, it may hide in the shadow of a minaret.

Buljanoff: And right now it's on the balcony.

Leon: They wouldn't let me in, so I had to get you out.

Ninotchka: Leon!

Leon: Ninotchka!
Ninotchka: So you're behind all this. I should have known.

Leon: Trying to keep me away from you! Why, as though that were possible!

Leon: Naturally I couldn't go on forever punching passport officials in the nose . . . but I found a way, didn't I?

Leon: Oh, darling, I had to see you. I wrote and wrote—

Leon: —and all my letters came back to me.
Ninotchka: And the one I got they wouldn't let me read. It began, 'Ninotchka, my darling,' and it ended, 'Yours, Leon.'

Leon: I won't tell you what came between. I'll show you. I'll prove it. But it'll take a long time, Ninotchka. At least a lifetime.

Ninotchka: Oh, but, Leon, I—I'm only here for a few days.

Leon: All right, if you don't stay with me then I'll have to continue my fight. I'll travel wherever there are Russian commissions. I'll turn them all into Iranoffs, Buljanoffs and Kopalskis.

Leon: The world will be crowded with Russian restaurants.
Leon: I'll depopulate Russia!

Leon: Comrade, once you saved your country by going back. This time you can only save it by staying here.

Ninotchka: Well, if it's a choice between my personal interest and the good of my country, how can I waver?

Ninotchka: No one shall say Ninotchka was a bad Russian.

Leon: Darling!

255

CAST

Ninotchka	GRETA GARBO
Leon	MELVYN DOUGLAS
Swana	INA CLAIRE
Razinin	BELA LUGOSI
Iranoff	SIG RUMANN
Buljanoff	FELIX BRESSART
Kopalski	ALEXANDER GRANACH
Rakonin	GREGORY GAYE
Hotel Manager	ROLFE SEDAN
Mercier	EDWIN MAXWELL
Gaston	RICHARD CARLE